MODERN LITURGY
HANDBOOK

MODERN LITURGY HANDBOOK

A Study and Planning Guide for Worship

Edited by

John P. Mossi, S.J.

PAULIST PRESS
New York/Ramsey, N.J./Toronto

IMPRIMI POTEST:
Richard P. Vaughan, S.J.
Regional Provincial, California

February 17, 1976

NIHIL OBSTAT:
Rev. Charles W. Gusmer
Censor Librorum

IMPRIMATUR:
Most Rev. Peter L. Gerety, D.D.
Archbishop of Newark

November 26, 1975

Library of Congress
Catalog Card Number: 76-12648

ISBN 0-8091-1952-8

Published by Paulist Press
Editorial Office: 1865 Broadway, N.Y., N.Y. 10023
Business Office: 545 Island Road, Ramsey, N.J. 07446

Printed and bound in the
United States of America

Contents

To my mother,
Ercelia,
for the many ways
she has taught me
to celebrate and enjoy
the liturgy of life.

Foreword

The Church of Christ has always been a pilgrim church, a church "on the way." It remains our task to constantly seek new and fuller expressions of worship. We should be glad that the worship experience continues to offer us challenge. In this manner our community prayer remains in process, alive, saved from stagnation. As a pilgrim people we are ever-developing, ever-discovering new dimensions of God in our midst. Of necessity, then, the articulation of this faith dimension of our pilgrim life must also develop, adapt, and redefine itself in our liturgy.

One of the perennial problems we face on this liturgical pilgrimage is communication. How can the expertise and wisdom of others shape our own liturgical expression? Faced with this question, a small group of enthusiastic liturgists decided to launch a mutual enterprise. The result gave birth to a resource periodical entitled *Folk Mass and Modern Liturgy* (now published as *Modern Liturgy*). The main thrust of the magazine is to blend the theoretical as well as practical aspects of worship. It is valuable to all people interested in good liturgy. The periodical provides a continuing source of background information, example liturgies, creative ideas, suggestions, and works of liturgical art such as musical compositions, dramas, dances, visual arts, and other special features.

Through its years of growth *Folk Mass and Modern Liturgy* now enjoys the recognition of a solid periodical for liturgical resources. But as every medium has advantages and disadvantages, there are some disadvantages inherent in the periodical medium. First, new publications must start small and grow, and so the early issues are missed by many who would enjoy and profit from their content. Second, while many copies of each early issue were printed, demand has caused supplies of certain issues to dwindle rapidly. Third, even though the content in each issue is relatively timeless, most people would not buy an old magazine copy. They would prefer another medium.

Father John P. Mossi, S.J. has happily produced a solution to these problems and has put together a publication which is excellent in its own right. This book is a logical extension of *Folk Mass and Modern Liturgy*. It provides an introduction to the planning process and a clear treatment of several of the artistic and environmental aspects of good liturgy. Fr. Mossi has selected and edited early arti-

1

cles from *Folk Mass and Modern Liturgy*, artfully arranged them for logical continuity and easy reference. He has added new articles where necessary to insure thorough and comprehensive treatment. The result is a volume which is self contained, instructive, and extremely useful as a practical source book for planners and leaders of worship.

WILLIAM J. BURNS
Publisher/Editor
MODERN LITURGY

Preface

Since Vatican II, a gradual liturgical reawakening has occurred in the Church. It has taken place on the national level, as witnessed by the increased interest in liturgical organizations and workshops, and on the local level, as seen in the countless liturgy committees that are now integral parts of the parish worship life.

As we can well remember, the first efforts to implement the new liturgy were embarrassingly awkward, something like a freshly hatched duckling that neither knew how to walk nor swim. In general, priests, choirs, and people (in those days, there were no lectors, acolytes, lay deacons, or extraordinary ministers of communion) were taken by surprise with the foreign liturgical language of English. Flaws became more apparent with each consecutive Sabbath disaster. Confusion abounded. The congregation no longer knew when to sit, stand, kneel, or strike their breast. New prayers had to be learned, and the complaint of the day was there was no time to pray—especially the rosary. Celebrants quickly found out that celebrating the new form of Mass according to the rubrical norms of the Latin Mass just did not mesh. It was like putting new wine into old skins; something sooner or later was bound to burst, either the liturgy, the priest himself, or the congregation. The similar early attempts of musicians to apply English psalmody to Gregorian chant was like trying to mix oil and water. All these signs screamed out the demand for a major course in liturgical education and retooling. Fortunately this rough liturgical period is for the most part behind us.

It is now in this second decade after the Council that celebrants, musicians, assisting ministers, and people are beginning not only to understand and appreciate the new liturgy, but also to feel at home with it. This slow process of becoming comfortable with the liturgy has taken much time for maturation. What the liturgy presently needs in order to flourish is a people who will continue to be committed to and care for the worship of the Church, enhance it with ritual, beautify it with song and music, and design appropriate space, vestments, and art worthy of its members, actions, and sacraments.

Modern Liturgy Handbook is a resource tool for those engaged in the work of planning and adapting the liturgy. It is a collection of contemporary articles which address both the structural theory of worship and the practical techniques of effective communication. The following chapters provide the liturgical principles, background, and

3

concrete suggestions for the celebrant, liturgy committee, high school or university student, seminarian, or interested laypersons who desire to acquire understanding and technical ability within the present liturgy's rhythm and structure.

The first chapters, Liturgy: A Perspective, and Theology Of Planning, which contain the newly published articles of James L. Empereur, S.J., provide a sketch of those historical movements that have influenced the present liturgy, and then explore the essential liturgical principles of good worship. Chapters three through seven address specific areas of the liturgy: preparation, environment, music, drama, signs, and children's liturgy. Chapter eight which treats home worship concludes the book. This last chapter is a deliberate statement that the what and how of worship must be integral with the totality of our lived actions, at church and home.

The contributors to *Modern Liturgy Handbook* come from diverse academic and pastoral backgrounds. All are actively engaged in the field of liturgy. Special thanks is due to three of the major contributors not only in recognition of their liturgical reflections but also for the support they gave to me in preparing this book: James L. Empereur, S.J., Professor of Liturgy at the Jesuit School of Theology at Berkeley; Reverend James Notebaart, Director of the Liturgy Office of the Archdiocese of Minneapolis-St. Paul; and Michael E. Moynahan, S.J., Liturgy Director at the College of the Queen of Peace in Santa Barbara. Lastly, Mr. William Burns, publisher/editor of *Modern Liturgy* magazine, is also to be highly commended for his incredible ability to bring together so many liturgists to express their ideas in one magazine. He has provided for many of us the paper and type with which to speak. Chapters three to eight of this book are a compilation of selected articles from *Modern Liturgy*.

May this book serve the People of God as a liturgical catalyst so that the important process of planning, adapting, and celebrating the liturgy can be done with greater expertise and facility.

JOHN P. MOSSI, S.J.
Our Lady of Sorrows Church
Santa Barbara, California

I
Liturgy: A Perspective

Where We Are at in the Liturgy

James L. Empereur, S.J.

Father James L. Empereur, S.J., an accomplished liturgist, has published a variety of articles on theological and liturgical questions, and has been an invited participant in numerous liturgical workshops. He is Liturgy Editor of Modern Liturgy Magazine *and Coordinator of the Institute for Spirituality and Worship at the Jesuit School of Theology at Berkeley.*

The present state of the liturgy could well be described as a luxuriant maze where even the expert would do well to walk warily. It would be the height of presumption to state where we actually are in liturgy. But as is the case with the rest of life the truth will be found in the middle of two extremes. And in liturgy we find at one end the irritated pastor saying with a sigh of relief that now that the liturgical books have been published by the Vatican, our liturgical reform is now over. It is completed. It needs only to be implemented. On the other side, we find such a distinguished liturgist as Godfrey Diekmann asking the question about our liturgical reforms: "Is it too little too late?"

The truth, I maintain, is in between. It is correct that we have come to the end of the liturgical reforms ushered in by the Second Vatican Council with the publication of such texts as the lectionary, calendar, sacramentary, and various rituals of the sacraments. But in fact, what we have is a new library, not a new liturgy. The liturgy found in these books does not respond to us who are Americans living in a secularized culture.

There is also some truth in the claim that these reforms are too little and too late. Many of the ritual reforms do not go far enough and those which have been implemented in the last few years are already in need of reform and adaptation. The addition of three Eucharistic Prayers to the centuries old Roman Canon of the Mass has only pointed up the inadequacy of a strictly limited number of these prayers. Steps have been taken to add Eucharistic Prayers for children's liturgies and some dealing with the theme of reconciliation. Much of the early legislation dealing with liturgical music was dated

7

the day it was published and one cannot help but wonder whether the reforms dealing with the breviary will actually restore the practice of a daily office in the Church or that the new rite of "going to confession" will prevent this practice from falling into oblivion.

But the picture is not all so depressing. There is a growing interest in liturgical planning on the grass roots level, a renewed interest in prayer with its concomitant effects for liturgical worship, the development of creative liturgical magazines, a hopeful sign on the liturgical music horizon, the organization of diocesan liturgical commissions and finally the formation of the North American Academy of Liturgy by professional liturgists for the purpose of their mutual enrichment.

There are several ways in which one can describe where we are at in liturgy. I shall focus on three: (1) the present scene in light of the entire history of Christian liturgy, (2) the stage of development of the modern liturgical movement in which we now find ourselves and (3) the contemporary liturgical situation as the confluence of many different movements in the Church as well as the end-product of several areas of renewal in theology that have influenced our liturgical thinking and practice. I turn now to the first perspective which will help us to see more clearly the direction that the renewal of the worship of the Church is taking.

The history of the Christian liturgy, especially as it has been concretized in the Roman Rite, can be divided into four major periods. There is the time which begins with the worship of Jesus and the early community until the end of the sixth century or the time of Pope Gregory the Great. This first period is called the epoch of creative beginnings. The period begins with the "sacred bridge" between the Jewish worship and the Christian liturgy. The liturgy of the Word, the Eucharistic prayer, the seven day week and the Church year all have Jewish roots. The Greek influence was felt in such things as exorcisms, anointings, the litany form and the ancient rhetoric. The second, third, and fourth centuries were the time of improvisation in the liturgy, the development of a catechumenate, lenten daily masses and the move from Greek to Latin as the language of the liturgy. During the fourth and fifth centuries the Roman Rite took final shape. In many ways this period is an obscure one in liturgical history, but at the end of it the substance of what we know as the Roman liturgy had come into being.

The second period of liturgical history which extended from the time of Gregory the Great to another Gregory, Gregory the 7th (c. 1073), was characterized by Franco-German leadership in the liturgy.

The Roman Rite took on its final form, many of the important liturgical books developed during this time, the liturgy of the hours came to completion, so-called private masses developed in the monasteries, a great deal of allegorization crept into the worship and diversity reigned in the liturgy (even in Rome). It is important to note the kind of journey the liturgy went through to produce the Roman Rite in the end. It started in Rome, then moved to England, then to France and Germany and then back to Rome. It is a fiction to think that the Roman Rite was developed solely in Rome, Italy. It is really a combination of many previously existing liturgies.

The period between Gregory the 7th and the Council of Trent is seen as a low point in liturgical development. It is the time of dissolution, elaboration, reinterpretation, and misinterpretation in the liturgy. The separation between the liturgy and the people that had been taking place for centuries previously now is finalized in this period. There is individualism in devotions, the liturgy is celebrated facing the wall, the canon of the mass is recited secretly, the structure of the so-called private mass influences the structure of the public celebration, the chalice is abandoned as a form in the distribution of communion, there is the multiplication of feasts of the saints, the meal aspect of the Eucharist is lost, there is the dissolution of the liturgical assembly as an assembly and the devotion to the blessed sacrament is more a matter of viewing than of receiving. Rome tried to counteract a number of these deficiencies by centralizing the liturgy and the Franciscans did the same by attempting to promote a unified liturgy.

The final period of liturgical history is that which covers the time from the Council of Trent (1545) to that of the Second Vatican Council. This can most adequately be described as the era of the rubricians. The breviary and missal are given their final form and the Congregation of Rites is established to decide on rubrical matters. There is little active participation in the liturgy although the Protestant reformers made attempts to make the liturgy more available by the use of congregational singing in the vernacular. However, the reception of communion did not noticeably increase among the Protestants. The Baroque period saw the introduction of additional ceremonial in the liturgy. The salient fact is that worship was simply not at the center of people's lives despite the Romantic attempts of the 19th century to revive interest in it. There was a decline in the Eucharistic living both among Protestants and Catholics. This period was really a continuation of the medieval influence. It was during this time, however, that the modern liturgical movement came into existence and flourished. And with the culmination of this movement in the Second Vatican

Council we have arrived at a new stage in the history of the Christian liturgy. But this stage can only be adequately understood if one has a sense of the development of the liturgical movement itself.

What is called the modern liturgical movement has been with us for a century and a half. Such an extensive period of time offers one the possibility of an overview which can more clearly delineate the various stages of growth in this movement. In order to determine where we are in the liturgical movement today, it is helpful to understand the nature and character of those steps which led to our present situation.

I divide the modern effort to change a once static liturgy into a dynamic, corporate worship of the people of God into four major periods: (1) 1832-1903, (2) 1903 - the Second World War, (3) Second World War to the Second Vatican Council and, (4) our own time. Such divisions have some arbitrariness about them and what elements chiefly characterized one period will be found to a lesser degree in the others.

The modern liturgical movement began in the 19th century. But there were movements of liturgical reform prior to this, such as during the Protestant Reformation. The present movement is characterized by its concern with the renewal as such. It is more than a by-product of another reform movement as was the case in the previous attempts to renew the liturgy. For the most part the present liturgical revival was brought about by the decadent state of the liturgy at the end of the eighteenth century. Eighteenth century liturgy was the logical result of the whole history of the liturgy: a story of the continual removal of worship away from the people. For instance, although the medieval age is one of growth of a liturgy whose main features had emerged by the 6th century, it was also the time of the dissolution and rigidification of worship. Liturgical worship became a clerical reserve. The Latin of the Mass had become a foreign language. The Council of Trent froze the Roman liturgy of the time, putting an end to any adaptation so necessary for further growth. The period of the Enlightenment was not favorable to liturgical reform because it lacked concern for history. But this situation became increasingly difficult to ignore as the Christian faith was under threat and as scholarship rediscovered the vibrant liturgical life of the ancient Church. It was Abbot Guéranger (1805-75) who almost single-handedly brought about the restoration that was to contain the germ of the liturgical movement of the twentieth century.

Prosper Guéranger ushered in the first stage of liturgical renewal which lasted until the pontificate of Pope Pius X. This period was one of recovery of the liturgical tradition. Guéranger and those who followed him in this work attempted to cut away the distortions and aberrations which had grown on the Roman liturgy. Their intention was to restore it to its pristine purity. In this way, so they thought, the liturgy would once again become meaningful for Christians.

Dom Prosper Guéranger launched the liturgical movement with the founding of the monastery of Solesmes known even into our own time for its work in the promotion of Gregorian chant.

He tried to bring the liturgy to perfection in the monastic setting. For him the ideal was worship as performed by the monks in their choir stalls singing the liturgy in aesthetic splendor. Much of Guéranger's liturgical theology is embodied in his monumental work, *The Liturgical Year*. But his achievements were limited because of his medieval and anti-Gallican tendencies. Influenced by the Romantic Movement in Europe, he viewed the liturgy of the High Middle Ages as the perfect form of worship. The tradition he attempted to recover was not that of the primitive Church but that of the thirteenth century. His emphasis on the Latin language and Gothic architecture is an obvious indication of his bias. His pro-Roman proclivities caused him to reject earlier French attempts to simplify the liturgy and make it meaningful to the people. He favored the Roman Rite to the point of denigrating the various Eastern rites. Nevertheless, whatever limitations may be found in Guéranger's work, his contribution has earned him the title "Father of the liturgical movement."

The influence of Guéranger spread throughout Europe and England. The German scene was influenced by the two monasteries of Beuron and Maria Laach. Two brothers, Dom Maur and Dom Placid, founded the first in 1892. Maria Laach was a daughter foundation from Solesmes. Both followed the Solesmes tradition in so far as their approach to liturgy was scholarly and archeological. However, they moved beyond Guéranger in that they did not limit their concerns to the medieval, but studied the Fathers of the Church in their attempt to rediscover the liturgical tradition.

The Belgian liturgical movement at this time emanated from the monastery of Maredsous founded by Dom Placid of Beuron. It emphasized the directly pastoral. One of the achievements of Maredsous was its vernacular translations of the missal for the laity.

The liturgical movement in nineteenth-century England was almost synonymous with the Oxford Movement. The name of John Henry Newman is a symbol of what this movement was all about. One of the aspects of this movement was the attempt on the part of certain Anglican clergymen to introduce more ceremonies into the lit-

urgy. They were accused of being crypto-Romans. The conversion of
Newman to Catholicism merely strengthened the conviction of those
who feared that those trying to renew worship were leading the
Church of England back to the papacy. But it would be a mistake to
view this liturgical renewal as primarily one of ritual and externals.
The movement was at its deepest a renewal of ecclesiology and spirituality.

One could characterize the nineteenth century liturgical movement as monastic, archeological, inclined to aestheticism, clerical,
non-didactic, rubrical and historical. This renewal of worship remained for the most part in monasteries scattered throughout
Europe. While it emphasized the importance of historical understanding for worship, it tended to turn the clock back to the Middle
Ages. Because this revival was still the reserve of the clergy rather
than an effort to restore the liturgy to the laity, it over-preoccupied itself at times with the details and beauty of ceremonies.

However, despite all these limitations, the nineteenth century attempt to recover the liturgical tradition reflected the theological renewal of that time as seen for instance in the work of such men as
Moehler and Scheeben. Biblical, patristic, and archeological studies
were assuming an importance which the liturgical movement could
not ignore.

The period between the reforms initiated by Pius X and the Second World War can be described as the time of the transmission of
tradition. This stage of liturgical renewal was characterized by attempts on part of the reformers to communicate the discoveries of the
previous period to the larger church. In fact, however, this involved
the clergy and religious more than the laity.

So important were the reforms of Pius X that some would begin
the present liturgical movement with him rather than Guéranger. In
1903 he issued a *motu proprio* (a special papal letter) in which he
launched the reform of church music and the restoration of Gregorian
chant in the liturgy.

In Germany, Maria Laach continued to work in the renewal of
Catholic worship under the leadership of Ildefons Herwegen (d.
1948). Its research was less romantic and medieval-oriented than
much of what marked the first stage of the movement. This monastery became well known for its liturgical weeks. It was the center of
European liturgical renewal from 1918 onwards. Maria Laach was
also the home of Odo Casel, probably the greatest liturgical theologian of the first half of the twentieth century. Casel was known especially for his work in "Mystery-theology," an attempt to explain the

reality of the liturgy in terms of the mysteries of Christ (i.e., his chief redemptive activities). For Casel the Paschal mystery was actually present in the mystery of the Eucharist. The saving actions of Christ that happened only once are present in the sacraments in such a way that the believers can re-enact them with Christ.

In Berlin, Johannes Pinsk, a student chaplain, promoted frequent communion and tried to relate the liturgy to the young. Romano Guardini, one of the great theologians of this century who made Germany his home, was interested in making the liturgy relevant to students by involving the congregation in the mass.

In Austria, at Klosterneuberg, Pius Parsch was concerned with the pastoral aspects of liturgy. He was a popularizer. His commentary on the liturgical year enjoyed considerable popularity for some time.

In Belgium, Père Lambert Beauduin (1873-1960), a monk of Mont-Cesar, really announced the beginning of the twentieth century liturgical movement on the occasion of the Catholic congress at Malines (September 23, 1909). The work of Mont-Cesar was ecumenical, connected to parish renewal and social minded in character. The famous St. Andrew missal was part of its attempt to disseminate the liturgy in the vernacular.

The Church music Society of St. Gregory and the Vernacular Society were indicators of the nature of liturgical reform in England. Here revival of worship tended to remain rubrical until the Second World War.

The Founders of the American liturgical movement form a cluster of well-known names: Virgil Michel, Godfrey Diekmann, William Busch, Gerald Ellard, Msgr. Hellriegel and H.A. Reinhold. Their work in the thirties culminated in the national liturgical weeks which began in the basement of a Chicago church in 1940. This coincided with the birth of the National Liturgical Conference. *Orate Fratres,* later known as *Worship,* began during this period. It is probably the best liturgical periodical published in the U.S.A.

In general one can describe this time of liturgical renewal as one that was less rubrical in character and more historical and theological in its emphasis.

The third major stage of the liturgical movement falls between the Second World War and the Second Vatican Council. It was characterized by the pastoral application of the tradition recovered earlier by the liturgical researchers and scholars. It is during this time that the earlier achievements of the movement are felt on the level of the local parish. The vigorous activity of this period is due both to official ecclesiastical approval as well as the expected spiritual invigoration following the World War. Pius XII published his encyclical on the Mystical Body, *Mystici Corporis,* in 1943. This was a forerunner to his encyclical on the liturgy, *Mediator Dei,* which appeared in 1947. This latter document has often been referred to as the *Magna Charta* of the liturgy since with it the liturgical movement in the Roman Catholic Church received official ecclesiastical approval.

This is the period when centers for research in the liturgy were established. In Paris the Centre de Pastorale Liturgique (1943) and in Germany the Trier Institute (1947) both pursued the scholarly investigation of the liturgy. Individual scholars made learned contributions, as for instance, Fr. Joseph Jungmann, S.J., who wrote the scholarly *Mass of the Roman Rite.* In the United States Fr. Michael Mathis started his liturgical school at Notre Dame University. This School of Liturgy is still the most prestigious in the United States.

Several important international liturgical meetings took place at Maria Laach in 1951, at Lugano in 1953 and at Assisi in 1956.

There was a great deal of rubrical and musical legislation during this time. Of special importance was the complete revision of Holy Week which began in 1956.

This period culminates in the *Constitution on the Sacred Liturgy* promulgated by the Second Vatican Council on December 4, 1963. It was the first document considered by the Council partially because so much preliminary work had been done by the liturgical movement during the previous one hundred and thirty years. The Council set up a liturgy Consilium whose purpose it was to implement its liturgical reforms: the updating of the Mass, the sacramental rites and other services such as the liturgical hours.

Although this was the period for the pastoral application of the liturgy, it, more than the previous two, was concerned with the relationship of theology to worship. Some of the major theological endeavors during this time were concerned with the nature of Christian worship, the meaning of the sacramental sign, the priesthood of all believers, and the relationship of individual to communal prayer.

We are now in the fourth phase of the modern liturgical movement. It is the period of post-Vatican II liturgical renewal. However, renewal is not an accurate word for describing this time. The three previous periods were times of recovery. The point was to re-discover the true liturgical tradition of the early Church and then to make this tradition pastorally feasible on the parochial level. It was mainly a time of restoration. But most of this work has been done. In the Roman Church the Consilium has completed its work and has now been combined with the Congregation of Rites to become the Congregation on Divine Worship. There will probably be no more major liturgical revisions coming from the Vatican. The task of liturgical renewal now falls to the national hierarchies with the final approval coming from Rome. This means that this stage is not one of restoration but of acculturation, adaptation, and experimentation. And if one can get any hints from the considerable amount of unauthorized experimentation that is going on (some of which is quite creative, some of which is clearly irresponsible), this will go in the direction of multiplicity in liturgical worship. This includes liturgies for different cultures and nationalities; liturgies for different age groupings such as for children, adolescents and senior citizens; liturgies for different situations: large groups, small groups, formal and informal gatherings. It seems that there will be more room for individual spontaneity and self-expression as well as extensive use of the multi-media.

One cannot predict the concrete results of this fourth period of liturgical renewal nor how long it will last. The time is yet too short to make any definitive judgments about the post-Vatican II stage of the liturgical movement. It will, I think, continue to pursue the main goal of the entire liturgical movement, namely, to restore to the Church its public worship so that the faith of the Church can be both expressed and reflected adequately.

Two important tasks lie before us who occupy this time in the history of the liturgy: (1) the implementation of the reforms put forth by the Vatican Council and (2) the adaptation of these specific reforms to various cultures. But the job does not stop there. There is the liturgy of the future to think about. That liturgy has yet to be created. Thus, there is need for real experimentation so that new liturgies can grow out of the contemporary religious experience. We are still adapting and acculturating our liturgy. Real experimentation has yet to begin.

Finally, it should be noted that this survey of the modern liturgical movement has omitted any reference to the revival of worship in the Protestant, Orthodox and Anglican Churches. This should not be construed as a judgment that the liturgical movements in these other communions are unimportant. In general, it can be said that their attempts to restore liturgy as the chief expression of the Christian community have developed along the same lines as the Roman Catholic movement. There are the corresponding four stages with very similar characteristics.

Before passing on to the third and last way of stating where we are in liturgy, it is important to make a few reflections on the *Consti-*

tution on the Sacred Liturgy. It is the most important liturgical document from the Catholic Church. It is both the embodiment of the great liturgical achievements of the past as well as an indicator of the directionality of the liturgy in the future. More than a passing reference must be made to it.

In brief, one can find in this document both a positive and a negative thrust. There are definite implications which follow from these positive and negative components.

There are three major positive characteristics of the *Constitution*. (1) It is not *only* juridical in character, but also pastoral, evangelical and theological. (2) It accepts in principle: change, adaptation, acculturation, diversity and intelligibility in the liturgy. (3) It emphasizes the importance of the secular mission of the Church.

The major implication of these three elements is that a radical change in Catholic piety will take place in the thirty year period after the Council. The late theologian, John Courtney Murray, said that the *Constitution on the Sacred Liturgy* would have the deepest long range effects of any of the Council documents because it affects peoples' lives of devotion. A change in liturgical piety will mean a very different kind of religious experience for Catholics in the future.

There are four negative components in the document. (1) There are elements in the document which were dated the day they were published, e.g. the chapter on liturgical music. (2) The document views liturgy too narrowly. It is equated with the official worship of the Church. (3) The document is insufficiently eschatological. The overly incarnational approach implies that anonymous Christianity leads to explicit faith. This is questionable at best. This perspective also implies that worship is the dynamic source of good activity. But it is not self-evident, as the document implies, that it is primarily in the Church's worship "that our redemption is exercised," and that it is here that Christ becomes chiefly present. (4) There is little concern for Christian personal and social ethics in the document.

The implications of these negative aspects of the Constitution are: (1) the document cannot be absolutized as were those of the Council of Trent or Vatican I; (2) its emphasis on Christian secularity undermines its own definition of liturgy which implies a clear sacred/profane dichotomy; (3) liturgy is not the summit and source of the grace-filled life in general, but of the Christian testimony to grace; it is central to what God does in and through the Church as a distinctive community but not necessarily central to his redemptive action in the world; and (4) Christians should regularly participate in worship, but not necessarily for their own sakes, but for the sake of their fellow Christians and the Church's testimony to the world.

So much for the historical approach to grasping our present liturgical situation. The more helpful and more comprehensive articulation of the present liturgical scene is the phenomenological one, the one that attempts to discern the contemporary liturgical context through a study of the various parallel movements of Church renewal as well as of the various theological disciplines and their impact on the liturgy. First, I shall review those movements running contemporaneously with the liturgical movement which have shaped and colored the revival of worship in the Christian Churches: the biblical revival, the ecumenical movement, the renewed emphasis on religious education, the revitalized study of spirituality and the awareness on the part of people of their historical relativity. Then, I shall deal with those areas of theology which touch upon our worship. The areas singled out here for consideration are: the theology of the Christian God, Christ, Church, sacraments, the human person and the end-time.

The five movements I have just mentioned have fed into the liturgical movement giving additional vitality and support as well as further specifying its task in the particular areas of the renewal of Christian living. Anyone who is concerned with the revitalization of worship in the Church must be acquainted with modern biblical scholarship and its implications for the regular liturgical services. Knowledge of new ecumenical liturgies, of the use of the liturgy as a teaching device in religious instruction, and of the relationship of liturgy to one's spiritual life is presupposed for those devoted to the liturgical apostolate. Since all are victims of their culture and since this present culture is very conscious of its historicity, those dealing with liturgical matters can hardly prescind from this in their dealing with the problems of worship.

But the traffic has not been only one way. In its turn the liturgical movement has added considerably to the work of the scripture scholar, the ecumenical theologian, the professional religious teacher and those engaged in spiritual direction.

Liturgy and the Biblical Movement

The work of the last century by so many scripture scholars, both Protestant and Catholic, has come to fruition in modern times. The new insights of these men and women have helped open the bible to many for whom it appeared permanently closed. While the many technical endeavors in the area of scripture studies are invaluable both for the advancement of these studies as a science and for their pastoral ramifications, what is of primary importance is that the biblical movement has restored the Word of God to its place in the spiritual lives of so many Christians.

A major effect of the biblical revival on liturgy is that there is a new appreciation for the entire bible. The importance of the Word of God as expressive of the Christian experience has caused liturgical reformers to place more scriptural readings in the services. This is obvious from some of the revisions. For instance, in the new Roman Catholic, Episcopal, Lutheran, and United Church of Christ lectionaries there are three scriptural readings for Sundays and feastdays of which the first is usually from the Old Testament.

The Old Testament is seen by Christians as the proclamation of God having its own value. Its primary purpose is not simply that which provides an introduction to the New Testament. Nor is it kind of a mine from which the New Testament can rob selections to suit its own apologetic purposes. This greater stress on the importance of the Old Testament in the process of the history of salvation has caused the Christian Churches to restore to public worship the place the Old Testament had in the early Church liturgy. There is more reading of the Old Testament in the liturgical assembly.

Since the Word of God comes to us clothed in the categories of another culture, it is necessary that it be explicated. This is the task of the biblical scholars. But all the efforts of these scholars would be in vain if the results of their work remained hidden because they were not communicated. For this reason, namely, that the Christians be really nourished with the Word of God, the place of the homily is now greatly emphasized in the liturgy. The homily is more than a supplementary comment. It is as integral to worship as any other element.

Liturgy and Ecumenism

It is difficult to imagine what the shape of the renewed liturgies of the individual denominations would be if there had been no ecumenical movement. All of the new rites have felt the influence of the desire for unity on the part of most Christians. This is especially obvious in the balance that one finds in the recent liturgical revisions in regard to the Word and the Eucharist. It is not facetious to observe that for the Protestants a large part of the liturgical movement has been the attempt to recover the centrality of the Eucharist, while for Roman Catholics it has been a re-emphasis on the importance of the Word.

To a lesser extent the influence of ecumenism on liturgical reform is seen in the area of common translations such as the *Glory to God in the Highest;* the *Holy, Holy, Holy; Lamb of God; Our Father,* and so forth. And not only do many denominations such as the Lutherans, Anglicans, and Roman Catholics share these common translations, they also have a common structure to their Eucharistic liturgy. For instance, Catholics who have participated in liturgies in the Episcopal Church frequently observe how similar the liturgy is to their own. The Consultation on Church Union, the organization of several Protestant denominations devoted to a continuing Church unity, has published ecumenical liturgies for both the Eucharist and Baptism.

There is much that the ecumenical movement can contribute to liturgical reform. This is especially the case in the areas of common initiation rites as well as liturgics that can be used for marriages between those coming from different denominations. How the various Churches can enrich each other in the areas of reconciliation, the anointing of the sick, and the ordination service has yet to be explored. But the greatest repercussions that the ecumenical endeavor will have on liturgical worship will be in regard to the question of intercommunion. Once there is even a minimal but official sharing at the Lord's table, there will be a growth in the public worship of the Churches that will be beyond our present imaginings. It is important to realize that intercommunion is not a matter of an individual's practice, but is a denominational stance between two or more denominations that the members of each denomination who are in good standing may receive communion in the other denomination's Eucharistic services. My receiving communion in the local Lutheran or Episcopal Church is not, strictly speaking, intercommunion since I do not speak for my denomination.

Liturgy and Religious Education

Liturgy is not primarily a pedagogical device. It is more the explicit celebration of something already present. One does not come to worship for information about the Christian faith, but to express unambiguously that faith to which one is already committed. What the religious educational movement has done is to help bring about this enlightened faith which is presupposed for liturgical celebration.

The liturgy can be defined as the community expressing its spirituality by means of symbolic involvement. If that is so, then the symbols of the liturgy must be self-evident. If one has to explain the symbol, then the symbol is not operative. This means that liturgy presupposes understanding. Christians must understand their common symbols before they use them to express themselves as members of the Body of Christ. Thus, while it is true that Christians learn much about their faith from the liturgy, the main communication of this revelation in its symbolic forms have to come from other sources.

What the liturgical movement has added to the educational one is the whole area of the experiential in the development of the Christian. Religious instruction is more than passing on information about certain facts. There are times in the evangelization process when words, doctrines, and propositions about the faith are without avail and it is necessary to make religious experiences available to the student. The liturgy fulfills that function and in this sense it is a catechesis. Communal assent to certain religious doctrines alone will not bring about Christian identification. This identification can only come about through the liturgy which is the celebration of the Christian past, present and future through common basic liturgical symbols.

Liturgy and Spirituality

Although the relationship of worship to the spiritual life is obvious, the real situation has been something otherwise. For centuries the schools of spirituality in the Christian community proceeded in a fashion parallel to rather than integrated in the liturgy. Some forms of spirituality in the Church were actually anti-liturgical. This tension between the two has lessened considerably at the present time. Contemporary spirituality sees the liturgy as the expressive climax of its own meaning and Christian liturgical reformers realize that liturgy is really the articulation of the spirituality of the community. This has aided the removal of the extreme individualism of much prior spirituality as well as an excessive objectivity formerly characteristic of the worship situation. Thus, one should not speak of private prayer as opposed to liturgical prayer. All prayer by Christians is the prayer of the Church. Some is more individual in character; some is more obviously communal. But none is asocial. This means that the liturgy serves as a criterion for the adequacy of different forms of spirituality. One obvious example would be that just as the Word of God receives priority in the liturgy, so it must in any form of individual devotion.

Both modern spiritual thinkers and liturgical theologians are anxious to relate both to contemporary concerns, to the human context where people are trying to live their spiritual and liturgical lives. Thus, both spirituality and worship are helping to overcome the extreme sacred/secular dichotomy which has so long afflicted the Christian experience.

Liturgy and History

Today people understand themselves as historical beings. They are always part of their cultural situation. As they pass from one culture to another, they do not remain the same. Change is very much part of human existence. To be a person means to be in process of becoming. The person is not transtemporal, transcultural, transspatial. And if the human person is constantly changing, then surely the liturgy must change. This means that revitalizing worship is more than simply trying to discover the original Church liturgy and restore it. The early liturgy was good for the early Church but it cannot simply be transplanted into modern times. The liturgy for today must be created. Moreover, liturgy must embody the process of change in itself. An unchanging liturgy is dead. It must be constantly evolving. If it does not, then in another hundred years it will be necessary to reform it again, to change it to a more contemporary form. This will then be accompanied by all the pain, anxiety, and identity problems that came along with the present reforms. In things that really count we change; we resist change in the area of sentimental attachments. What person refuses a colored TV because it would mean a change from the black/white picture? Who refuses an increase in salary because it would mean a change?

Another value that the emphasis on our historicity has contributed to the liturgy is that the place of the history of salvation is more clearly seen in the Church's worship. The history of salvation, which is human history viewed in light of the fact that salvation comes to us through this same history, is summed up most explicitly in the liturgy. In the liturgical assembly we have the meeting of the past, present, and the future: the entirety of salvation history. In the liturgy the story of revelation as it has come to us in the past is commemorated, the workings of God's self-revelation in the present time are specifically celebrated, and the culmination of this history in Jesus Christ is anticipated. That revelation is not abstract truths, but the story of events is brought home more obviously in the liturgy than any other place.

LITURGY AND THEOLOGY

Almost all the areas of renewal in theology have had some influence on liturgical theology. This is not surprising since liturgical theology is really the worship aspect of all of the other theological disciplines.

Theology of the Christian God

There is a growing concern on the part of ordinary Christians as well as theologians to view God as working very closely in people's lives. God is not seen so much as a completely transcendent being, one who is "out there," or "over against us." God is very much part of human history. He is the one who is giving the direction to the process whereby we are becoming more fully human. The Christian God is seen as a changing God in that he is constantly drawing all of history into himself. He is calling humanity to assume responsibility for itself and so achieve salvation by becoming more of what it should be.

With such a view of God, the liturgical assembly becomes the place where the presence of this God is brought to high expression. God is in the midst of the praying people. It makes sense for the priest to face the congregation because in addressing his prayers to God the Father he is addressing the people of God who make up the focal point of the mysterious presence of God. In the past when we viewed God as someone "up there," or "outside of us," it made sense to have the priest face away from the congregation. He was leading the people in prayer to God who was "before them." But now that we see the liturgy as a celebration of the fact that God is the deepest dimension of our lives, the priest is not viewed so much as the mediator between God and ourselves as the one who presides over the community's ritualizing attempt to allow God to rise to visibility.

Theology of Christ

The key discovery of modern Christology (theological study of the meaning of Jesus Christ) that has changed liturgical thinking is the centrality of the Resurrection. In the past, the cross was viewed as the unique act by which Christ redeemed the world and the resurrection was seen as a kind of confirmation of that sacrifice. With the deepened realization that the resurrection is as much a salvific event as the death on Calvary, we can understand that the Christ that is present in the liturgical actions is the Resurrected Christ. There is no other. The cross is important, but so is the resurrection. The cross becomes meaningless except in terms of the present Risen Christ. The cross and resurrection are to be kept together. They are the Paschal Mystery. It is this mystery which is expressed and articulated in liturgical worship. And this Paschal Mystery is the Christ who is living, who exists as risen. When this mystery present in the liturgy was seen in terms of the cross alone, the emphasis was on the past event especially in terms of its sacrificial nature. Recall the universal reference to the Eucharist as the "Holy Sacrifice of the Mass." But our liturgy is not a celebration of the Christ of the past only. True, the liturgy is a commemoration of the great events in the life of Christ which went into making him the kind of person he is now, but it is the present Christ who does the worshipping in the liturgy. He now offers himself to the Father as he did by dying on the Cross, by rising from the dead and by ascending to the right hand of the Father. The centrality of the resurrection in the liturgy is highlighted by the realization that the crucifix as the normal sign of Christian salvation is at worst, an anti-sign, and at best, unliturgical, except, of course, its use on such specific occasions as Good Friday.

Another point that contemporary Christology has emphasized for liturgical practice is that Christ is the subject of the liturgy, not primarily the object of worship. Worship is to the Father, through Christ and in the Holy Spirit. Jesus gathers up our worship and joins it to his and then brings it all to the Father. If Christ were not doing the worshipping in the liturgy we would not have Christian liturgy. One of the problems with the traditional benediction service was that it tended to focus on Christ as someone to be adored rather than as someone to whom we are united through a meal. Christ was seen as the object of the worship rather than the subject who by means of communion is uniting the Father and the worshipper.

Our contemporary understanding of the Risen Christ does not restrict him to any time or space. Christ is truly and really present in all of creation. But there are certain situations in which Christ's presence is more clearly and unambiguously expressed. The *Constitution on the Sacred Liturgy* reminds us that Christ is really present in the liturgical assembly, in the proclamation of the Word, in the Church's ministry and in the Eucharist. These are all real presences. However, the method of expression is different. One is not less real than the other, although the degree of Christ's presence differs as does any human presence. The Eucharist is more explicit in articulating the presence of Christ than is the assembly gathered to celebrate the Eucharist. Christ's presence is like married love. It is the same real love present in the wife's washing the dishes, in the husband's giving his spouse a gift on the occasion of a wedding anniversary, and in the act of sexual intercourse. But some of the actions highlight more obviously the meaning of married love than others. So it is with the liturgy, that clear and unambiguous sign of the Church.

Theology of the Church

We are more aware today that the Church is a sign or sacrament. It is the clear expression of the meaning of Christ in people's lives. It is not so much that the Church is the place of salvation as it is the focal point of that salvation which is taking place in the world under the direction of God wherever we are becoming more fully human. Just as Christ is the sacrament of God, the unambiguous sign of the presence of the Father in the lives of people, so the Church is the sacrament of Christ saying something clearly about how Christ is working in the world.

The liturgy is to the Church what the Church is to Christ, an explicit proclamation of its meaning. In this sense the liturgy is the Church in the concrete. The liturgy *expresses* the meaning of the Church. That means that in the liturgical assembly you have an adequate reflection of what the Christian community is all about. All the elements which are necessary to make some community to be Church are found in the gathering of Christians for worship: the presence of the community, the proclamation of the gospel, the ministry of the Church and the celebration of the sacred banquet of the Lord. In this sense the liturgy reflects the Church.

Liturgy as the proclamation of the community also constitutes the Church. The Church is brought about by the presence of Christ and since Christ is present in the liturgical proclamation, the Church is created through it. The liturgy proclaims by means of the community gathered for worship, by the preaching of the gospel, by the work of the ministry and by the Eucharistic sharing. These are the very elements that make the Church be Church. And when you have the assembly expressing itself through these various elements, you have the Church, because what the Church is has been brought to the level of ritual expression. In this expression there is deepening, growth and advancement. In this sense liturgy constitutes the Church.

Since liturgy is the reflection of what the Church is, it is the model or paradigm of the meaning of the Christian community. It is the Church most the Church. I do not mean in the sense that Christians are most Christian when they are at the liturgy. They probably engage in their most Christian activities outside the worship situation. But it is liturgical worship that clarifies the meaning of their lives as lived in the Church. It is what lights up for Christians and mankind in general the meaning of Christ in the world, namely, that God is drawing all creation to union with him. It removes the ambiguity from any area of their communal living in Christ which could be misunderstood or be confusing to others. Therefore, the liturgy must faithfully reflect the faith of the community. It raises that faith to the level of clear expression and it promotes that faith which is intensified in its being raised to higher consciousness.

The conclusion of what has been said regarding the relationship of liturgy to the Church is that worship presupposes community. If you have no community, you can have no liturgy. Many parishes have deficient liturgy, not so much because the celebrant is poor, the musicians inadequate, and the environment detrimental to worship, but because there is no real unified community that can celebrate its existence. If there is ever to be a meaningful parochial liturgy, there will have to be some drastic changes in the parish structure and life.

Theology of the Sacraments

There are two key insights from contemporary sacramental theology which have profited the liturgy immensely. The first is that the sacramental situation is one of personal encounter. No longer are the sacraments to be seen as impersonal means of grace in which all that is necessary is to go through the rite without placing any obstacle in the way in order for God's grace automatically to follow. Now sacraments are viewed as events in which the entire person is ritually involved and which facilitates the kind of encounter with Christ which characterizes people meeting together in community with some depth. This means that the liturgy is not simply something objectively done before us which we witness and from which we profit. Rather, worship is celebration through symbolic action, and because symbolic action is human action, liturgy is always the action of human beings. The liturgical act cannot be divorced from the human context. Our redemption is highlighted through sacred signs, but this can only mean that God's presence is more fully articulated by the fact that there are real red-blooded people engaging in certain forms of human activity which cause them to reveal themselves more fully. In this transparency that occurs in ritual involvement, God is more existentially disclosed. That means that God is humanly disclosed. One becomes transparent and naked to others through personal activity. The degree that I have revealed my Christian experience to others is the degree that I have revealed God to them. God is personally revealed in a community's self-transparency. That is what liturgy is all about. It is the communal disclosure of God in Christ by means of human symbolic involvement.

The second insight of sacramental theology so important for the liturgy is that sacraments (and here I mean the liturgical rites) are celebrations of a reality already present. The being of the sacramental situation does not begin with the liturgical ceremony. This situation is a process of which the liturgical celebration is a necessary part. For instance, one's sins are forgiven before the priest pronounces absolution. They are forgiven as soon as one turns to God. The sacramental rite is the thanksgiving of the fact that one has been reconciled with God and that this reconciliation is completed in one's being reconciled to the Church. Again, one is actually married before pronouncing of the vows. Marriage begins when there is unreserved commitment between two people to spend their lives together. The ceremony is a necessary part since this union must be expressed in a public way or it will die. You cannot keep something on the implicit level a long time and expect it to grow. For example, you cannot say that you love someone but that you never intend to express it in any way. Such a love is a truncated one that will soon wither away and die. What all this means for the liturgy is that worship is to be seen as bringing to the level of heightened awareness the reality of one's experience of being Church. One is part of the Christian community long before one liturgizes. One is Church between liturgical celebrations. Such celebrations are not magical moments producing the Church on the spot as it were. They are, however, indispensable since the reality of the Church would be distorted and lost unless it is expressed in terms of praise and thanksgiving.

Christian Theology of the Person
     The theology of what it means to be human, sometimes referred to as Christian anthropology, is concerned with what it means to be a person in light of the Christian faith. Among the many insights which contemporary thinking in this area has highlighted and which have importance for the liturgy, let me note two:
     (1) What does it mean to be human? There is probably no real answer to this question, but what we see more clearly, as many Christians have always known, is that humanity is the focus of the divine. There is no real unbridgeable discontinuity between God and us. We are manifestations of God. By that we mean that people in their depths are radically religious beings. To be fully human means to be God-like. Mere humanism is not good humanism. To speak of humanity in opposition to God is to speak of humanity superficially. "The glory of God is the person fully alive."
     This means for our liturgy that it must be a fully human one. We cannot pretend that worship is for God rather than people. Nor can we excuse what so often goes on in our churches by asserting that sacred worship is to be separated from the rest of human living because it is directed to God. Worship is to God, but for people. And it cannot be to God if it is not for us who are the human concrete moments of God's presence.

(2) The meaning of grace and sin. The tendency today is to view grace not as a thing, a substance, or an accident, but as a relationship. Grace describes one's orientation to God as sin is a symbol of one's disorientation away from God. A loving relationship between oneself and another human being is the closest analogy we have at our disposal for speaking about grace and sin. Grace is not a thing and sin is not an act. They are descriptions of tendencies.

Thus in liturgy it is not terribly meaningful to speak of getting sanctifying and actual grace from the reception of the sacraments. They are heightened moments of a relationship already there, a relationship that is graced when it is intensified and which can be weakened and obstructed by sin. Individual actions are ambiguous. They are more or less evil depending on their effect upon the relationship as well as how they articulate the tendency of the relationship. To speak of a specific sacramental grace from a specific sacrament should not be viewed as getting a certain soda flavor out of a particular fountain. Sacramental grace simply means that our relationship with God which is very complex is celebrated under a certain formality in a particularly important situation in our lives: baptism, marriage, anointing, etc. Liturgy does not produce grace from nothing. It brings it to visibility in a cultic form.

The Theology of Eschatology or the End-Time

What a renewed theology of Eschatology has introduced into Christian living is a new sensitivity to the fact that this life should include a tension that is pulling one toward the end-time. We live in the expectation of the coming of Christ and what that will bring. Actually, the new order has been introduced by Christ. We already live in a new creation. In this sense we live in the last days. The second coming of Christ will fully disclose the new order that is now only partially revealed. This order gives direction to our present lives. Because we already share in the Risen life of Christ, this new order is not something which we get only as a reward after our death. Nor do we share in the death and resurrection of Christ merely as individuals. It is given to all of us as a group and so the Church is an eschatological community of hope: one that lives the risen life but incompletely and is on the way to a fullness of this divine life. Christians who have an awareness of the end toward which God is directing all things will take a larger view of their religion. They will not reduce it to an affair of individual happiness. They will realize that part of their task of salvation is to help bring the whole world to union with God.

For the liturgy this has meant the re-emphasis on the aspect of the future in our worship of God. Our liturgy is an anticipation of that final liturgy which will be celebrated at the end of time. Now it is only incompletely that. This is a literary way of stating that there is a tension that is pulling it toward that final goal. Our liturgy is on the level of a new order, but only in a beginning way. Liturgical celebrations are not just commemorations of the past or articulations of the present. They are also a pledge and foretaste of the future glory of which the resurrection is the sign. We gather together in the liturgical assembly to await in hope the second coming, the end-time, the final union of all creation with the Father. Because our Christian experience is future directed, sacraments (for example) are to be seen more as eschatological events than celebrations of past occurrences. The past is not depreciated; the future, however, is to be given greater emphasis since that is the direction in which we are moving.

Conclusion

An invigorated study of the scriptures, a new ecumenical spirit among the Churches, a revival of the proclamation of the gospel, a deeper understanding of the spirituality of the Christian community, a greater sensitivity to the person as an historical creature, a more processive view of God, a reemphasis on the significance of the Risen Christ, an insight into the mystery of the Church, a richer and more personal view of the sacraments, a more positive perspective on the human, and a reawakening of eschatological hope: these are some of the present roots of the modern liturgical movement. There are others which could be mentioned. But these are the main ones and the list is sufficient to indicate that in the liturgical movement one is dealing with a very extensive renewal that is not limited only to the narrow confines of public worship. Liturgists are interested in far more than just ritual changes. They are seeking to spread by the renewal of worship the vast reorientation of the Christian experience that is taking place as exemplified by the various trends that feed into the liturgical movement. What is taking place in this modern movement to restore the liturgy to its rightful place in the Church is really an extensive pastoral renewal in the whole Christian community.

II
Theology of Planning

Liturgy and Secularization

James L. Empereur, S.J.

Raimundo Panikkar in his book, *Worship and Secular Man,* has said this: "Only worship can prevent secularization from becoming inhuman, and only secularization can save worship from being meaningless." That statement sums up the underlying principle of this article: which is, (1) that we are living in a secular age and unless we worship by means of a secularized liturgy, we will not be articulating the contemporary religious experience, the only kind of religious experience we can have today; and (2) that it is possible that a secularized society can forget to refer to the religious dimension of life at all, and so it is necessary that we be a worshipping people so that our liturgy can sit in judgment on our culture.

I do not intend this article to be theoretical in nature, but more pastorally oriented. However, it is appropriate to define my two terms—worship and secularization—since we all approach the question of worship in a secularized society with a number of presuppositions which can very easily confuse and muddle what I am hoping to make clear.

For the sake of discussion, I take Panikkar's definition of worship: namely, that it is any human action symbolizing belief. Not every action is worship, but only those which are the expression of religious beliefs. I am sure that most of you would find this acceptable as a comprehensive definition of worship. But the meaning of secularization is more difficult to ascertain. The secular refers to this world of space and time. On that we can all agree. But there are many different ways to understand the meaning of the process of secularization since this understanding is based on the kind of value we place on time and space. For instance, one can consider life in this time and space in a negative way. People who do this make a distinction between the secular world and the sacred world. And it is only this sacred world which is important. The spatio-temporal is transient, the sacred is everlasting and so only the sacred is worth a real investment of our energies and beliefs. For people who look at life with this kind of dichotomy, secularization can only be a regrettable phenomenon: the invasion of the unholy into the realm of the religious.

31

But there are those who consider this life of time and space in a very positive light. The secular is seen as the arena where people become full human beings, assuming their responsibilities and overcoming prejudice and all that would divide life into hard and fast categories of thinking and doing. For people who so view life, the process of secularization is the discovery of the real depth of our time and space.

In the first view of those who make a sharp distinction between the holy and profane, the sacred when applied to liturgy means that some person or thing is a manifestation of the holy. This can be understood properly, but there is a danger here. It can happen that chalices, candles, vestments, and the clergy become so sacred as to take the place of God functionally speaking. In the past we have at times so "sacralized" the ministers of the liturgy, that they became identified with Jesus Christ himself.

The second view of secularization does not wish to get rid of the holy. But it objects to absolutizing any person or thing as the manifestation of God. In other words, to secularize here means to repeal every effort to absolutize what is considered holy. Secularization in this sense means not to abolish the sacred but to restore it by bringing out its relativity. For example, Church authority must be de-sacralized (secularized) when it has become so sacred as to make itself as unquestionable as God. Persons and things are desacralized when it is pointed out how they symbolize and are ordered to something beyond themselves.

There is a concern today to desacralize liturgy, to secularize worship, to relativize what is a finite experience, namely, the articulation of our spirituality or Christian liturgy. There is no attempt here, however, to reduce liturgy to life or vice versa. To quote Panikkar again:

"To convert the whole world into a temple would not do, and to identify the temple with the world at large would not solve the problem either. If everything is worship, then nothing is worship. In other words, there has to be identity, on the one hand, and difference, on the other."

But so much for the theory. What does this mean practically for one's view of worship and for liturgical planning? I would like to make several points characteristic of a secular society and show what each one means for liturgy on the practical level:

1. A society in process of secularization is liberating itself from

religious authority. I doubt that that statement needs any further proof. For those who accept it no proof is needed; for those who do not, no proof is possible. Ecclesiastical authority especially no longer enjoys its previous unchallenged and privileged position. What this means for the liturgy is that worship cannot be a one man/one woman show. The liturgical leader does not command respect and influence just because he or she happens to be ordained or in charge of this particular liturgy. They must have earned their authority. A liturgical leader should not be imposed upon the worshippers, nor should he or she force their own understanding of the Gospel upon their listeners. God's communication to us in worship does not simply come from above. He speaks through the community also. The priest can be more adequately described as the one who articulates the community's experience of the transcendent rather than one who brings God to their midst. That is why it is necessary that the liturgical symbols employed today enable one to encounter Christ through the faith of the community, not just through the mediation of the priest. It is true that the hierarchical order of the Church (whatever kind of structure this may be) must be reflected in the structure of the liturgy, but such an expression is difficult to bring about because of the present rejection of triumphalism. Yet the ecclesial structure can be concretized in the liturgical framework when it is seen as a question of differentiation of roles of various kinds of service.

2. A society in the process of secularization is characterized by a constant re-examination. The point here for the liturgy is obvious: experimentation. But experimentation for a secularized liturgy must contain the elements which should be found in any authentic contemporary experiment:

(1) The absence of adequate structures should be recognized and admitted. The present rites are not doing the job.

(2) In default of adequate structures new forms are to be sought in a systematic way. Experimentation is not play or innovation. It is an interdisciplinary and scientific search.

(3) It belongs to the methodology of experimentation to fix its duration. If there is no time-limit, it ceases to be experimentation.

(4) Likewise essential for a methodological experiment is reversibility. If one cannot go back to former structures, one is not experimenting. One has already opted for changes.

(5) The experimental project, before being carried into execution, should be submitted to the authority of the respective community. Authority here refers to more than the leader of the community. The baptized, mature Christian possesses authority in the Christian community also.

(6) An approved experimental project should be carried out methodically with its consequent advantages and disadvantages. Do not change the experiment in midstream so that you manipulate the results.

(7) Regular reflection on the evolution of the experiment is required. We are not speaking of underground liturgies where the experience of each liturgy passes into oblivion.

(8) After final reflection, an experimental idea which has proved satisfactory should be integrated as soon as possible into the structures of the liturgy. Anything else would be less than honest.

I would like to suggest some areas where we need liturgical experimentation today: (1) Religious language. Can scripture communicate in the form in which it is given to us? The present normative liturgy presupposes that the modern believers have the mysteries of the faith available to them in their biblical expression. But is that the case? Is not contemporaneity sacrificed for doctrinal security when it comes to the question of articulation of the faith in worship? (2) How symbolize the transcendent today? To what degree should the sacred/secular tension be overcome in order to do so? (3) Should today's liturgy reflect the technological age or rather our frustration with it? (4) Is it possible for us, for whom a token meal has no secular significance, to celebrate the eucharist as we do now or must it be replaced by a more obvious meal? (5) What forms of prayers of petition and intercession should be used in a world in which we are becoming more and more responsible for ourselves and which is more and more in our control?

3. A world in process of secularization thinks functionally. This means that there is less interest in the nature of being than in becoming, less interest in God's omniscience, omnipotence and his other abstract attributes than in what he has done and is doing in human history. For the liturgy this means that we worship the specific acts of God rather than the more generalized conceptualizations of divinity. It also means that there must be greater concreteness in the liturgy, e.g., naming the sick for whom you are praying, not praying for

peace, hope, joy, etc. in general, but peace, hope, and joy in a specific context.

In the preaching, in the prayers, the profession of the faith and the confession of sins, the worshippers are not interested in only general historical realities, but want to come to grips with the actual society in which they live.

This functional approach to liturgical worship implies the rejection of the aesthetic symbol in itself as the apt indication of divine presence. For instance, Gothic cathedrals and Renaissance polyphony do not automatically serve as signs of transcendence. There is also the rejection of the artificially mysterious. The creation of an aura of mystery around liturgical celebrations by contrived means such as as unintelligible language no longer is an effective symbol of God's presence. In place of the aesthetic apparatus, people today are more satisfied with the sounds and objects of daily life in which they must live out their Christian experience. That is why there is a demand for a less formal atmosphere and genuine awareness of one's neighbor in the liturgy today.

This functional approach to liturgical worship demands the use of intelligible symbols because only such symbols can convey the personal presence of Christ. Thus there should be a real immersing in water in baptism, there should be real bread in the Eucharist, there should be children's liturgies for children, and there should be more domestic celebrations of the Eucharist.

The functional aspect of a secularized liturgy does not allow for the over-sacralization of persons and objects employed in the service. For instance, vestments and space are not sacred in themselves but only by their use for religious purposes. Nor is function necessarily indicated by externals alone such as clothing, e.g., pontifical vestments do not speak clearly of the function of the bishop in the Christian community. People challenged by gospel-values today do not want other-worldly symbols that separate their worship from daily life.

Times of worship must follow the rhythm of modern society. Already this rhythm is changing because the seven day week is disappearing. The four day work week is gradually becoming a reality. The week-end is a time-away rather than a time at home. What does that say about Sunday worship? Is it possible that Sunday is becoming the worst time for the community to assemble for worship? Is it realistic to attempt a regular weekly liturgical celebration for the whole community? Would something like the pattern of ten Christ days during the year (some would reduce it to 3 or 4) in which the whole local church would worship together, this being supplemented by regular weekly domestic liturgies, would this be more feasible in the future? We are in the middle of a cultural process and so no solution in any one place will be universally valid.

4. A secularized world does not place a great deal of emphasis on the tension between the sacred and the profane. The society in the process of secularization is more interested in stressing the continuity between the holy and the secular than the dichotomy between the two. For contemporary liturgy this means that the relationship of the sacred and profane should be seen as an incarnate reality where in actuality the two are not distinct. This raises the question of what kind of symbols can be found in such a liturgy. Secular liturgy (if I may use that term) does not mean doing away with symbolism. But it does raise the question: what kind of symbols are indicators of the divine for people today? In other words, what can symbolize today the unity of the faith and hope in the worshipping community?

The answer to the problem of symbolism in a secularized liturgy is not found in creating new single symbols, like substituting a strobe light for the Pascal Candle, but rather in the growth of a new ensemble of objects, acts and symbols. If we tried to substitute symbols which we find irrelevant with others we may find more fitting, we would be doing the Christian community a great disservice, because past experience has shown that the community would simply invest the new symbols with the old meaning. It is impossible to invent new symbols. The symbolic forms of worship must be redone as a whole and not by bits and pieces.

This new symbol-set should have the positive result of doing away with superstition and emphasizing the true nature of sacramentality. The sacred which this symbol-set would communicate should be the religious depth dimension of all creation. The function of worship is to make us more sensitive to these depths. It should focus, sharpen, and deepen our response to the world and other people beyond the point of proximate concern to that of ultimate concern, to employ Paul Tillich's language. The liturgy is the proclamation, the adoration of the holy in, under, and with the common or secular. The profane is not to be viewed as the godless section of life. Rather if the profane/secular terms have any meaning they should refer to the world as cut off and alienated from its true depth.

If the sacred/secular tension is stressed too much there is the danger that the liturgy will create a world of its own. If the tension is simply ignored, there is the possibility that people will try to escape explicit worship by taking refuge in some social crusade. This is ultimately self-defeating since the reform of society can never progress beyond the personal condition of those who constitute the society. This tension must always be present because we cannot escape the state of humanity with its fragmentation and lack of personal wholeness. But we must also see the liturgy as the explicit celebration of Christ who has triumphed over human estrangement and the demonic in the world. Panikkar nicely summarizes the point when in echoing the sentiments of the Dutch theologian, Edward Schillebeeckx, he says: "Secularization represents the regaining of the sacramental structure of reality, the new awareness that real, full human life is worship, because it is the very expression of the mystery of existence."

5. The negative aspect of secularization, the departmentalization of religion and worship, the separation of liturgy from life, must be avoided. This is not a problem peculiar in our time with its concern to secularize the liturgy. We have perennially had the problem of the fact that Sunday worship had nothing to do with the rest of the week. But in our time the focus has shifted. Now the problem is whether the preceding week has anything to do with the liturgy on Sunday. Is our weekend celebration an articulation of what has gone on the six days before? This can only happen if the symbols used in the liturgy are closely linked with our ordinary life in the world, symbols which can help disclose the depth of meaning in all human existence. The tendency of people today is to see Christ when they share with their fellow persons a sincere, genuine, and unselfish desire to be of service to the weak, the destitute, and the poor. The symbols in the liturgy must contain a real awareness of the suffering presence of our fellow persons; they must help raise the dignity and worth of each individual. They must symbolize the faith and hope of the worshipping community and this must involve no escapism or withdrawal from the realities of daily living. On the other hand, the liturgical symbols must also recall clearly and without apology the Paschal Mystery, especially the death, resurrection and exaltation of Christ. They must prefigure the future hope of the liturgical community. As already noted, no single sign can accomplish all of this. Rather the ensemble of symbols must bear this responsibility.

These are some of the aspects of the secular world which must be considered when speaking of worship for people today. Perhaps I can summarize what I have been saying in this way. There are three elements which are necessarily involved in any Christian liturgy: (1) The historical Christ-events which are made sacramentally present in the liturgical celebration however which way this is to be explained philosophically; (2) the signs and symbols through which these events or mysteries of Christ are present; and (3) the living community in which they are made present. Secularization of the liturgy is a process which affects numbers two and three, but never number one. Secularization, as I have defined it, would never deny the reality of the Christ-events sacramentally present. Rather, secularization leaves the first element intact and is concerned with the signs and symbols as well as the community through which the saving events of Christ touch the contemporary worshipper.

In this article I have been almost exclusively concerned with the second element: the signs and symbols which communicate the saving presence of Christ. But the fact is, that I have not touched on the deepest problem in the matter of secularizing worship which is the third element of Christian liturgy: the living community which employs these new and old signs and symbols. After all, before we can have a secularized liturgy in terms of new signs and symbols, the second element, we must have a secularized, living community ready to express itself in terms of these signs and symbols.

But in order to have such a community, one must have one that prays, one articulating its contemporary experience of the Christ-event. That is why, ultimately, the question of the secularization of the liturgy rests upon the alleviation of the problem of prayer today. One can increase the general quality of ritual celebration, and one can attempt to allow new symbol complexes to grow but both of these presuppose a faith community of praying people.

The first task then toward secularizing the liturgy is to study the Christian community's prayer, concentrating on the humanizing aspects of such phenomena as: cursillos, better world retreats, charismatic prayer meetings, small group shared prayer, or the more well-known traditional forms, prescinding from the overly individualistic piety, simplistic views of community and deficient Christian anthropology which is often found in these prayer forms. Only then will it be possible to discover the kinds of symbol-sets that will be adequate for a liturgy in our contemporary culture. If liturgy articulates the community's spirituality, the secularization of worship means beginning with that spirituality.

Liturgy in an Electronic Age

James L. Empereur, S.J.

There is without any doubt in my mind a malaise that characterizes the contemporary liturgical movement in the United States. This is puzzling for many since most of the forms of our worship have been updated according to the criteria of the Second Vatican Council, namely, pastoral relevance and continuity with the original forms of the early Church liturgy. Nevertheless, these revisions have not produced the renewal of Christian living so longed for by the pre-Vatican II liturgical pioneers. Some liturgists today even suggest that these reforms have come too late. Whether or not they are correct in their prognosis the fact is that we have moved into a new period of liturgical revival after the Council. Until the promulgation of the Constitution on the Sacred Liturgy, we were concerned with the restoration of our liturgical tradition. Now we must occupy ourselves with adaptation and experimentation. This must be a time of creativity or our liturgical movement will die. We are seeking a liturgy, or better, liturgies, yet to be created, ones which go far beyond the forms that we have today. In this sense the recent revisions of our liturgy are already out of date. If the liturgical movement is to regain its momentum, it must transcend our present liturgy.

One of the keys to understanding the future shape of the liturgy is the environment. We are more and more aware of our surroundings and their influence on us. Previously, we saw ourselves as apart from our environment. It was something we conquered and controlled. Today, we see that we are partly constituted by our surroundings. They so permeate our lives that we develop within the world around us in a way that we cannot be separated from it. This does not mean that we are completely determined by it, but it does imply that for the person to grow and become more human, he must interact with his environmental context. He cannot simply reign victoriously over it. It is not his to possess. It is his with which to dialog. So, if we are to find forms in which the person can express himself adequately in terms of his communal experience of the Christ-event, we must consider the environment. We have a new world now and we cannot do the job demanded by this new environment with structures and rites which worked for a previous environment.

What most characterizes our new environment is change or process. And the medium of this process is electronic technology. We are more shaped by the nature of the media than we are by the content communicated by the media. We are totally involved in our media and when they change, we change. Think, for instance, of riding in an automobile rather than walking. In the car one moves more quickly, but also with greater detachment.

The old environment was mainly one of vision. Our power of sight was intensified to the detriment of our other senses. The importance placed on vision was brought about by the discovery of the alphabet which depends only on the eye for understanding. The subsequent invention of printing simply confirmed and strengthened this stress on the visual. This emphasis on one sense damaged the unity of human experience. For instance, the portable book, which is a result of printing, created the situation of people reading alone and so becoming detached and noninvolved. Again, industrialization and the factory assembly line fostered the idea of specialization which in turn encouraged greater detachment since a specialist need only use a part of his abilities. Marshall McLuhan describes this environment of the past with the emphasis on the visual as "hot." This means that one sense was "heated" up to the point of monopoly over the others. The result was that the degree of human participation in the environment was cut down.

Although there may be serious problems in accepting uncritically McLuhan's thesis about the modern environment, still some of his insights are helpful in dealing with the liturgy. Here I would like to acknowledge my debt to two important articles dealing with the McLuhan thesis and the liturgy. They are: "Liturgy Hot and Cool," by Thomas F. O'Meara, *Worship,* Vol. 42, No. 4; and "The Liturgical Medium in an Electronic Age," by Charles C. McDonald, *Worship,* Vol. 44, No. 1. What these authors and I find especially pertinent in McLuhan's work for liturgy today is his distinction between hot and cool media. I am not implying, however, that my conclusions in regard to the liturgy and liturgical planning springing from my analysis of the relationship of the liturgy to the contemporary environment would be endorsed by Marshall McLuhan. The opposite might well be the case.

One might quarrel with McLuhan's specific examples as to which media are hot or cool, but nevertheless, his general approach here is very helpful. A hot medium for McLuhan would be something like the radio, a movie, or a photograph, while the telephone, TV, or a cartoon are cool. A hot medium is one that brings a single sense to "high definition." High definition means to be filled with data. There is very little left for the viewer to fill in. For instance, a telephone is cool and a radio is hot because in the case of the telephone the ear is given so little information. A cartoon is cooler than a photograph because so much must be supplied by the viewer. Speech is cool because so much has to be supplied by the listener. Hot media are low on participation while cool media demand more audience involvement. When you compensate for what is not given, you get involved. A lecture (hot) has less participation than a seminar (cool) and a book (hot) less than dialog (cool). McLuhan applies these categories to all the media of communication.

It is McLuhan's contention that from the time of the discovery of the printing press until our own, our culture has become more and more print oriented. As a result, the visual was heated up. Since the environment of an age is shaped by the media and since the patterns of peoples' lives are created by the environment, it was to be expected that the liturgy became highly visual. The obvious example of this was the former solemn high mass which was a feast for the eyes. One should not automatically condemn that development. It was the best pastoral response that could be made at that time.

This overemphasis on the visual in the liturgy, this overheating of the sense of sight, produced a liturgy that was low on participation and involvement because in the heating up of one of the senses, there is fragmentation. The primacy of the visual causes fragmentation because things must be broken up. The eye can see things only one at a time. There is noninvolvement as far as the total person is concerned. In the case of the solemn mass, apart from the incense, there is the participation of one sense alone. It was not by accident that this time of emphasis on the visual in the liturgy was also the time when there was greater interest in passively viewing the consecrated host rather than receiving it.

The intensification of the visual environment had caused the structure of the liturgy to lose its equilibrium. In Protestant worship, it meant such an emphasis on preaching and the liturgy of the Word that the Eucharist and other forms of symbolic sacramental activity took a definite subordinate place in the liturgical assembly.

We are still very much addicted to the visual in our worship. Whereas formerly we were spectators at what approached at times the dimensions of religious drama—the solemnity of the mass—now we are like a group of people crowded into the same library all reading copies of the same book. People still feel more comfortable reading the liturgical readings and the Eucharistic Prayer from their missalettes no matter how well they are being proclaimed by the priest. But the laity are not the only ones still in the Gutenberg era with its preoccupation with the printed page. The ministers in the sanctuary read the texts as if they were reading a book privately, rather than proclaiming that message which can never be identified with something printed on a page. The publication of the new sacramentary has only intensified the problem. Some celebrants are so tied to the text that they read everything in black including the prayers meant to be prayed quietly. Another example of how the visual emphasis has influenced liturgical practice is seen in the present-day reluctance for community singing. Song is very involving for the whole person and a print-oriented congregation is uncomfortable with that much involvement.

Print tends to stress the individual's own point of view. This creates a congregation of people who are each engaged in their own kind of devotional activity. The individualism which is still present among many worshippers colors the way they deal with silence in the liturgy. Moments of silence are not situations of interaction among the members of the congregation allowing God to speak to them as a group. While we are experiencing the end of those times when they occupied themselves with other forms of activities such as their own prayers which were not directly concerned with the liturgy, we still get the distinct impression that for a large segment of our congregations silence is a time of uneasiness and embarrassment.

In an atmosphere that overheats one aspect of human knowing, there is a tendency toward uniformity and rigid classification that stresses an isolated specialization and is lacking in a sense of wholeness. Certainly, our older liturgy was very much the same everywhere and there was a preoccupation with rubrical details to the point of stifling worship itself.

Now, however, we are moving from the world of print and sight to that of the electric circuit in which things are sudden and simultaneous and where there is instant feedback and so a greater sense of the total human experience. Thus, we need to study this environment. We need to detect the way the media are influencing us so that we can understand their import for liturgical planning. Since the liturgy is a medium of communication, and since communication takes place in an environment, in an electric environment, we need an electronic liturgy. In our age of technology the visual principle is hardly adequate for the expression of worship.

The real problem with the liturgy today in terms of the McLuhan thesis is that we have a hot liturgy in a cool generation. More and more people, not only the young, want immediate and intense involvement. This is not the kind of involvement that comes from a great deal of information or data. People are not interested in more systems or ideologies.

Involvement, which is what McLuhan means by cool, comes not so much through informational content as by significant experiences and lasting human commitment. For those who are at home in the electronic world, the message comes through imagination and person-stimulating relationships rather than speculative analysis and logic. This is the reason there is so much disenchantment with the abstractions whether they be found in books, homilies or pastoral counselling. For the message to come through it must be experienced.

The experienced message is not a comprehensive one. It is always limited. It is never grasped in its totality and so it remains a partial communication. A "cool" person becomes highly involved by responding in a restricted area. Our needs are limited; our power to grasp is finite. This limitation allows involvement to be concrete and authentic. Because the experience is circumscribed, it can be effective. If one's involvement is too generalized, then it is greatly diminished. One cannot become involved in the whole Grand Canyon environment all at once. One cannot grasp the whole history of salvation in a single instance. A cool society finds small combos more involving than a Handelian chorus accompanied by a gigantic orchestra.

With too many words, with an overcrowding of ideas, the liturgy becomes unreal. It is pure information. It centers on itself. But if liturgy is a situation of proclamation and response, if liturgy is a dialog between God and the person, if God interprets himself as God and humans interpret themselves as Christians in the liturgy, then it must be a medium that allows for an experience which can only be described as a communication-happening. This requires a high degree of involvement. A complex, preachy liturgy will not do this.

Maximum involvement will only take place when the visual and the tactile equal the verbal, when spontaneity complements the programmed elements and when there is movement and dance as well as stationary moments.

Dialog homilies, the use of slides, movies, drama, dance, mime and recorded music are all ways of introducing the media into worship. They can have a cooling effect on the participants.

For instance, one of the reasons the guitar is popular in contemporary liturgies is that it merely suggests. It is a cool instrument and demands more participation, whereas the Baroque organ is a hot instrument since it gives everything and leaves little for the input of the participant. The listener is passive.

The liturgy must speak a limited message. Thus thematically, the liturgy should focus on one area through all its elements such as the readings, the music and the presidential prayers. The liturgy's theme must be more than hope, love, peace, or joy in general. To fashion a lasting liturgical experience it must be a particular kind of hope or love that is celebrated. This has tremendous ramifications for the readings in the liturgy. In a cool liturgy we must be existentially involved in them. But this is only possible if there is some limitation exercised. This means that there are too many readings in the liturgy. While there are distinct advantages in the three readings for the Sunday liturgy, in general, I feel that this approach is disastrous. Apart from the fact that the middle reading rarely has anything to do with the Old Testament reading and the gospel which are tied together thematically, the amount of verbalization that we now have in the liturgy means that there is a further depreciation of the symbolic aspect. Not every thing need be said in every liturgy. The homilist should not attempt to cover the entire history of salvation every time he preaches. It is simply a matter of celebrating a particular liturgy for this particular group.

Another one of the necessary prerequisites for bringing about a unifying focus in the liturgy is that there be more spontaneity. The prayers of intercessions are a good example here. Usually, when they are done spontaneously they refer more than adequately to the theme of the liturgy and serve as an involving, unifying element in the whole celebration.

The important point in all this is that we are called upon now to study the liturgy as a medium. We must understand its impact and its effects. Only if we do this will we be able to avoid overheating the liturgy either in our planning or conducting of such worship. Most of us whether as priests presiding at the liturgy or as those who are engaged in the preparation of the liturgy in some sense are still too concerned with the content of the service and do not recognize that liturgy is primarily a medium. Not to respect this primacy is simply to add a different content to the old visual liturgical pattern. The major problem with the so-called thematic liturgies is that the theme has been seen almost exclusively in terms of informational content and not in terms of the medium.

Our traditional liturgy, and I include the present normative mass, is low on personal involvement because it is too high in content. It is overheated because it is repetitive; it has an unchanging structure; it dictates the responses and so lacks spontaneity; it is filled out by means of information. The liturgy tends to be impersonal because its content is not decided by the local community but by a universal liturgical calendar. One can only enter into the Roman liturgy by first entering an *a priori* structure. The fact that the present normative rite now offers the opportunity of one or more options in many places does not exonerate it from the limitations of an overheated liturgy. Nor would adding ten or a hundred more dictated options convert it into a liturgy for McLuhan's global village.

I do not wish to insinuate that cool liturgies are good and hot liturgies are bad. It seems that for some hot liturgies are necessary. I am thinking here of children in lower grades. They need more input, more ideas, stories and the like. Nevertheless, our major liturgical problem today, as far as the electronic world goes, is moving from a print-oriented, verbose, rubricized, rigid, non-involving liturgy to one that is cool and that can be entered into existentially. And this is possible only if the liturgy is limited in its emphasis on the visual, in its use of words, in its structure, and in its content. This liturgy will be more involving.

I would like to sum up in several points the determining effects that the electronic environment is having on the liturgy and which will have to be considered in any kind of liturgical planning and adaptation.

1. Because of the instantaneous character of the electronic media, the greater mobility of people who live in the electronic environment, and the more circumscribed area of "cool" response, there will have to be more diversified groups to meet the needs of more specialized kinds of involvement. For instance, François Houtart has suggested that the liturgical assembly should be divided into small groups (4-20), the assembly, and the crowd. And each liturgical grouping would have to have its own liturgical structure. The same rite will not work for these three different sociological groupings. That is a large part of our present problem. The Roman Mass was designed for the assembly which met in a basilica style Church. It was never meant for the small group liturgy. A domestic or home liturgy of about a dozen people takes on an air of stiffness and overformality when the presiding priest feels that he must stick to the normative mass rubrics completely. And this is no wonder since the normative mass was only intended for a church assembly of several hundred people.

Another area affected by this greater flexibility in the groupings and by the mobility of modern people is that of the responsibility for planning and celebration. The clergy and those directly involved with the liturgy will have to plan much more carefully and in greater detail. Nor can one presume that the congregations are going to be fairly homogeneous and that a more generalized liturgical format will fit them. Rather, each celebration will have to be handled with an eye to the particularity of the situation and the worshippers involved. No two congregations will be at the same stage of development and so the Sunday celebrations in the parishes will be evolving at their own pace. With the gradual change of the territorial parish and the blurring of geographical boundaries there will be much more passing from parish to parish and this will influence the particular style of liturgy to be found at a given parish at a given time.

2. Because electronic media tend to decentralize and counteract uniformity, there will be greater variety in the forms of the liturgy. Obviously, then, what we look forward to is not a new rite, but new rites. Already certain countries such as India and Japan on a very restricted scale are adapting the Roman Rite to their culture so extensively that one could begin to speak of national rites. But this acculturation must go further than the national scene. We need more than an American Rite. Even under the large umbrella of an American liturgy, different forms will develop, whether in terms of different parts of the country, different professional and age groups, or those responding to special occasions.

Outside of the Eucharistic liturgy, the electronic environment with its emphasis on flexibility and variety will mean that Christian initiation will no longer be able to be done in a uniform fashion for all at all times and places. Each should be allowed to approach his formal liturgical integration into the Christian community at his own pace.

3. A new medium tends to employ older forms which it then transforms in such a way as to allow for the possibility of creativity in contemporary expression. This is what has happened in the liturgy. Up to the time of the Second Vatican Council our concern in liturgy has been one of restoration of the early tradition of the Church which was then adapted for pastoral purposes. But now we are moving beyond that. In this present period of the liturgical movement the emphasis is on creativity and acculturation. We are more interested in the liturgies that are to be created than in the liturgies that are to be revived. For instance, the new Eucharistic Prayers of the Roman Rite are not really new at all. They are a paste-and-scissors job of older formularies. For this reason, they are to be considered transitional. Just as Prayers Two, Three, and Four will eventually overshadow Prayer Number One and let it sink into oblivion, so newer and more contemporary prayers will eventually replace these three. This point is that since people who come from the electronic background accept

change as normal to life, the elements of the liturgy must be open to change.

In our present period we will have to create the kind of atmosphere in which our most innovative people will be able to experiment. It is questionable whether this experimentation can ever take place in large groups. For this we must start with small groups of real communities who are celebrating their lives. The only alternative to experimentation is to turn the task over to those who will rush in and engage in it irresponsibly. Often I am asked by many people acquainted with my work in liturgical experimentation, including a few bishops, how I can justify what I am doing. They are especially concerned because I am a professional liturgist and theologian and they feel many will follow my example. I have only one reply. I try to show my students and those who seek my liturgical advice what I consider responsible experimentation to be. If I do not do it, they will simply go off on their own and the liturgy and the worshippers will be the worse for it. My holding the line, my refusing to experiment is not going to stop others from engaging in it. Only the naive would maintain that if we all hold the line, the aberrant experiment in the liturgy will go away.

4. A cool liturgical environment should be looked upon as a work of art. And as art it becomes the detector of changes that are taking place in the life of the Church. Because the environment of the liturgy can give us some indication of which way the wind is blowing in the Christian community, it can be considered a teaching machine. Without reducing the liturgy to a purely didactic device, it is possible to utilize it for religious education. By that I mean that a liturgy which does not acquiesce in the production-line mentality, that does not try to produce identically shaped worshippers to become part of a great liturgical machine, will educate people to explore and learn about the changing life processes.

5. Each liturgical celebration should be a specially programmed event. It should be unique in terms of its planning and preparation. Many would object to this. They say that to try to make each liturgy creative and so different in some way is to turn it into a show or a futile attempt to do something different every day. They object that this does not fit into the rhythm of our lives which are by and large along the same pattern from day to day. The difficulty with this objection is that it is based on the notion that the Eucharistic liturgy is a daily celebration. It is not for most. To try to make each daily celebration such as found in religious communities something different than that which preceded it the day before would be intolerable and ultimately

unproductive. We cannot have a unique event each day. But it is the weekly celebration we should be concerned about. Daily liturgies need a certain amount of sameness, a sameness which is due more to their simplicity rather than their repetitiveness. For many daily liturgies, a reading of scripture with some meditation, sharing, and praying, with a brief Eucharistic Prayer and communion rite—all lasting about twenty minutes—is something both feasible and desirable.

6. The electronic age demands a greater interplay of the senses. We have only started to develop the forms that will give greater involvement to touch, taste and smell. We have begun with such simple things such as using real bread in some of our liturgies—bread that tastes and smells and feels like real bread, and not fish food.

Even when participation is at a maximum, the use of the sense of touch is minimal. There is very little physical contact in the rite with either the objects used in the service or with one's fellow Christians. We have made a very hesitant beginning of introducing the human body back into worship by the gesture of peace and various forms of liturgical dance. But think of the difficulty the kiss of peace is having in so many parishes. Yet touching things and persons changes worship. You cannot remain a spectator if you touch. In the early Church when the person to be baptized was stripped naked, led into a pool of water which covered the major part of his body, was generously anointed with oil and was clothed in a new white garment, it must have been impossible for that person to remain uninvolved. He was participating with his entire body.

Each liturgical environment demands its own degree of bodily involvement. A full bodily embrace done without hang-up or reserve may be out of place in the local congregation of 700 people, but in small-group liturgies of those closest to you anything else would be inauthentic.

7. The most important element in any multimedia is the person. Media are channels through which ideas and experience flow between persons. "Good media is like dialog, not monolog." The images that appear on the screen cannot remain there. They must come off of the screen and dwell within the people. So, an electronic liturgy is not one where the sounds continuously bombard the ears of the worshippers, but rather where the sounds are so organized that the listeners become involved in what is heard and even help shape the sound environment. Mixed media are not the same as multiple sensations. Barring those ever frequent technical difficulties, most multimedia liturgies which do not work fail because the planners did not make that distinction. An electronic liturgy is one where there is the interplay of electronic media and the human person.

Liturgy as Proclamation

James L. Empereur, S.J.

It is my strong conviction arrived at through a great deal of experience in liturgical planning that all attempts to revive worship today or to make liturgy a meaningful part of the whole effort of the pastoral renewal of the Church must presuppose an adequate theoretical foundation. In other words, there must be a clear and well-defined liturgical theology underlying one's adaptation and acculturation of the liturgy. One cannot continue to introduce new forms of worship, exploit the mass media in different sacramental situations, engage in more personalistic encounters à la the various group sensitivity methods and the like without a solid theological underpinning. Invariably, this lack of an adequate liturgical theology will lead to new distortions and aberrations. All the balloons in the world, all the smiling priests in the country, all the warm embraces at the kiss of peace will not make a liturgy be what it should be: the place where the Church becomes the Church.

What is a theology of worship? It is a theology of how the Church becomes Church. We cannot speak about liturgy until we know what it means to be Church. If it is correct to say, as liturgical theologians do, that the liturgy reflects and constitutes the Church, that is, worship expresses and actualizes here and now in a concrete symbolic situation the nature of what the Christian community was, is and will be, then those who work in liturgy must know what they are trying to reflect, what they are trying to actualize and constitute. The liturgical planner must have a firm understanding that what the liturgy does is to show what the Church is and at the same time to help the Church to become more Church. The purpose of liturgical worship is to direct the Church to its present task of being that clear and unambiguous sign of what God is up to in the world and to urge the Church forward to that shape that it must have at the end of time.

Because the liturgy reflects the reality of the communal Christian experience and is also the self-constructive activity of the Church, it cannot be separated from the community. Liturgy presupposes community. If there is no real community, there is no liturgy. But it does more than bring to expression and create the Christian community's experience. It is the articulation of the spirituality of that community.[1] Worship manifests and deepens the faith dimension

49

of the Church. Rites, rituals and formulas express and form the spirituality of the community. Liturgy deals with the vision of a community, the conditions of a community and the faith of a community.

But what is that spirituality of the Church that the liturgy brings to visibility and intensifies? The meaning of this spirituality is basically the Christian community's relationship with God. But in order to get at the meaning of that relationship it is important to note that people relate to others and so to God in terms of their self-image. For instance, someone who sees himself as worthwhile and as being loved will relate to God differently from one who sees himself as hateful and without value. Thus, we can say that the Church's spirituality is its self-image of who it is. Since our self-image is what we are in fact becoming, liturgy is, then, the expression of what the Church is actually becoming.

But how do we know what the self-image of the Church is? We know it through the process of self-transparency. For instance, we experience this transparency in the prayer groups that are springing up around the country. In these, people let themselves become clear to each other in their faith dimension. They show each other what makes them Christians. And what makes them Christians is becoming the People of God in terms of the vision of Jesus Christ. People who share this vision want to celebrate it. It is in liturgical celebration that they let this vision become transparent and thereby place themselves in relationship to this vision.

Self-transparency means shared vision. For instance, we all know people in our lives whom we are inclined to trust because of the way that they conduct themselves, interact with others and allow what is going on inside of them to come through to us. The natural tendency is to reciprocate by opening up our own interiority and letting them enter more deeply into our lives. This brings about union whether it be that of a good working relationship with your mailman or whether it be that of a deep love between two friends. In either case, for there to be reciprocity, there must be transparency, there must be some shared vision. And through this mutual self-exposure, one affirms one's self-identity, one's self-image.

The self-image of the Christian community is brought about by the self-transparency of that community. And that transparency is the sharing of a common vision by all the members of that community. And the vision they share is the Risen Christ himself. This Christian vision is the primary ingredient of the Christian self-image. It is by means of this communal self-image that the community relates to God. In other words, its spirituality is in terms of this self-image.

And since liturgy is the articulation of the community's spirituality and since liturgy is this communal faith-transparency brought to the level of ritual awareness, the Christian liturgical assembly is the self-image of the whole Christian community raised to the level of explicit communal activity. Liturgy, then, is the articulation of the spirituality of the Christian community because it ritualizes in communal symbolic activity the self-image of the same community. This group self-image is constituted by the shared vision, the communal faith, and the mutual self-transparency of the members of this community. And what they share, believe in common and reciprocally expose to each other is that they have been, are and will be the People of God in the Risen Christ. This kind of intersubjective action that goes on in the human dynamic of faith-sharing brings about the ecclesial reality that we call the Church. As Christians expose their relationship to God and to other people in a ritualized situation they become more what they are; they become more the People of God. They assert more and more their self-identity, an identity that is founded on the Resurrected Christ.

What this means on the pastoral level is that liturgy should never be primarily a question of the techniques of liturgical planning but should always refer to the transparency of the faith aspect of the community. The fundamental criterion of liturgical planning is the facilitation of the faith dimension of a particular community. What does this say about the faith of the president of the assembly? Must he/she assume more than he/she actually has? Does not the need for transparency argue for the necessity of non-verbal forms of communication? Can the present normative Roman Rite allow for sufficient transparency in small groups? Can we continue to hide behind ritual, afraid to expose the deficient faith that may be there, when true symbolic and ritual involvement means self-exposure?

The importance of shared vision among Christians is that such sharing allows them to be present to one another. It is in their mutual self-transparency that God comes to visibility. And when what is shared is belief in the Resurrected Lord, it is Jesus Christ who comes to presence. Presence to one another through shared vision means being present to the world. There are those in that world who claim there is no ultimate meaning to life. We proclaim there is meaning for us. Because we share the vision of life's significance, suddenly the world is confronted with a group of persons filled with hope. Our prophetic witness to the world is achieved by the authenticity of our vision. If we forget our vision after the celebration, our liturgy is inauthentic.

Liturgy must be more than the cementing of a fragmented group into unity, however. It must manifest that human history is the progressive movement by God revealing his own intersubjective dynamic with the world. Thus, lying behind contemporary liturgical theology is the basic notion that it is creation itself which is revelatory of God's salvific activity. The whole world is a sacrament in this sense. The purpose of Jesus Christ is to clarify for us that what God is doing by utilizing all creation for the purpose of ultimate union with him is not uncharacteristic of God. God is very much in character in drawing all people to him through their becoming more fully human. Jesus Christ is not unique because he alone brings salvation. He is unique because he is the chief exemplification of what God is all about, namely, that salvation is achieved through the world and people becoming what they should be. Jesus was the perfect religious man. By his life of love and goodness and especially by his great sacrifice on the cross and his victorious resurrection he made it clear that all forms of love, goodness, sacrifice and resurrection are salvific. In this sense, Jesus is the great sacrament of God.

And so too with the Church. The Church is a sign or sacrament. It is to Jesus Christ what Christ is to God the Father. It is the clear and unambiguous sign of what Christ is all about. It has no monopoly on salvation. But it is a witness to meaning, to the fact that Christ has stated in his redemptive activity that God is working in the world wherever the world is becoming more and more what it should be. This is another way of saying that the Church is the sign of the incarnational activity of Christ in the world. The world must deal with a group of people who believe, who find in their transparent sharing all that makes their lives significant. It is in this sense that the Church is a sacrament. But this does not mean that the Church or the Church's liturgy has any monopoly on achieving union with God. It is the world rather than the Church which is the primary place of salvation. The Church is not the usual place of salvation. It is the focus of that salvation which is taking place through the whole process of this world's becoming. Rather, the Church is the extraordinary place where salvation takes place. Most people have not been saved through the Church, most are not being saved through the Church and there is little hope that most people will be saved through the Church. The Church is that symbol of what Christ is all about, but clearly and explicitly so.

What we have said about Christ and the Church can be said about the liturgy. What Christ is to God the Father, the Church is to Christ and the liturgy is to the Church. The liturgy is the unam-

biguous articulation of what it means to be Church. Just like the
Church, but more specifically, the liturgy remembers and celebrates
the great things that God works in the lives of men. Just as the
Church is the focus of Christ's meaning and activity, so the liturgy is
the focal point for the action of the Christian community. The liturgy
is the clearest statement that can be made about the Church. Not that
most of us are most Christian in the liturgy. I suspect that the opposite is the real situation, but it is in the liturgical assembly that
something is done which can have no other meaning but Church.
Other good Christian activity such as social work can certainly be
redemptive, but it can also be understood in such a way that it does
not clearly say something about how God is drawing the whole world
to himself by the attracting power of his all-encompassing love. For
instance, a Christian working in the inner city is doing something
which certainly can bring him to God and salvation. But that aspect
of his work may not be uppermost in his mind. Nor would it necessarily be so interpreted by the people with whom he is working. Many
would understand what he is doing as purely good human activity. He
himself could lose his sensitivity to the transcendent dimension of his
work. In brief, the liturgy is the Christian community's *proclamation
to the world* about its own meaning: that all men and women can be
brought to union with God by becoming better people. The liturgy is
the proclamation of the Church because the Church is the proclamation of Christ and Christ is the proclamation of God.

But what is it that we mean by the word, proclamation, when
applied to the liturgy? Surely we mean more than speaking in sten-
torian tones. It must be more than merely talking. Proclamation
would have little connection with our liturgical experiences if it only
meant giving information as one does in verbal communication. No,
proclamation is much more than that. Proclamation is language, but
not any kind of language. It is certainly more than the usual language
that we speak every day. It is what theologians call a language event.
In order to understand what we mean by liturgy as proclamation we
must first analyze what is meant by language-event, how this concept
applies to our understanding of liturgy, and finally what are some of
the practical results which flow from this definition of Christian worship.

Language is more than the words we use. It is part of our existence and reality. We live in a world of meaning which has been given
to us by language. And by language I mean not only words, but all
forms of human communication such as gestures, movements of the
face, music, art, dance and inflicting violence as well as making love.

Language, in this broad sense, is the way in which human beings communicate and become present to one another. If there were no language, there would be no human presence and if there were no human presence, you could not talk about reality. If you are standing next to someone in a crowded bus, you might well be physically present to him, especially if he has his elbows in your back. But you are not personally and humanly present to him until you turn around and say something. There is a sense in which our *personal* reality is constituted by language. We live in relation to others to the degree that they are present to us and they have revealed themselves in language to us and we to them. We could not live if there were no language (in the broad sense). Just imagine how empty our lives are when even one kind of language is missing. The inability to talk or see is obvious in its limitations, but suppose that there were no kissing in human activity. There would be one entire aspect of human affectivity which could never come to presence: that dimension of human love which can never be communicated in words, even poetry, or in some other form of human touch or symbolic involvement.

When we speak of proclamation as language, whether it be verbal, visual, or tactile, we are concerned with proclamatory speaking. Proclamatory speaking is a way of pointing. This pointing allows us to bring meaning into the foreground. By speaking, we detach and connect meanings; we analyze and synthesize. Proclamatory speaking permits the one who is pointing to go beyond the limits of time and space. The speaking word is the creative world. It changes reality. It helps constitute our relationships. Our world is constituted by the assembly of words and persons and things that have meaning for us.[2]

In the musical, *The Man from La Mancha,* the knight-errant encounters the local whore, Aldonza, at an inn which for him, of course, is a castle. He sees her as a lady and so gives her a name representing that ideal, Dulcinea. The old man amuses Aldonza but she is also caught up short and calls him her greatest tormentor because he has shown her what she might have been. This is painful. At the end as our hero lies dying, Aldonza and Sancho arrive on the scene. A bystander challenges her for wanting to comfort the old man. The people call her Aldonza. "My name," she says, "is Dulcinea."

It was not just a sound that changed Aldonza to Dulcinea. It was the faith and the vision of the knight-errant. Not that the word was unimportant. It was everything since what happened could not have taken place without the word. The word was more than the communication of information. It challenged Aldonza to a new vision of reality.

This calls to mind the biblical union of word and action. G. Van der Leeuw in his *Religion: Its Essence and Manifestation* says:

> Whoever speaks, therefore, not only employs an expressive symbol but goes forth out of himself, and the word that he lets fall decides the matter. Even if I merely say "Good Morning" to someone I must emerge from my isolation, place myself before him and allow some proportion of my potency to pass over into his life, for good or evil. . . The word, then, is a decisive factor; whoever utters words sets power into motion.[3]

In his *The Phenomenology of Language*, Rémy Kwant speaks of words as a way of "pointing." When we point at someone with our hands or nod in his or her direction, that person has a meaning he or she would not have without the pointing. Kwant says that our culture does not look kindly on people who point toward the infirmity of the cripple. "If they do it anyhow, his deformity begins to exist in a new and more striking way both for himself and for others. Pointing raises a meaning out of its relative concealment."[4]

Kwant uses the distinction between the speaking word and the spoken word. Ordinarily we use spoken words, but when we are creative and challenging we use speaking words. In the march on Washington in August of 1963 when Martin Luther King, Jr. gave his "I have a Dream" speech, these words articulated a vision that the hearer had to make a decision about. This was a case of the "speaking word." What King meant by what he said would not have been real in the same way for those who heard him had he not spoken in the way he did.

In this way words can take on special importance in the human community. They depend on the community and yet the community lives by them. A community is formed when people can assent to the "speaking word." They share what is expressed in the speaking word. This word itself comes from within the community and is not an external force. However, since communities are not just groups of people who get together often, but are composed of those who share a common vision and a common language, it may not be possible today for the speaking word to be effective on the parish level. It may be that we will have to look for more natural groupings which have common understandings for friendship and joint endeavors.

The fact is that we all live in community and as members of some kind of community we all live in some language context and tradition. Most of us live in many communities: family, club, church and so live in many language contexts. Some time ago, in a liturgy in St. Ignatius Church in San Francisco, the celebrant of the mass during the breaking of the bread used the words of Jesus as recorded by St. John: "Your fathers ate the manna in the desert and they are dead; but this is the bread that comes down from heaven, so that a man may eat it and not die." In the congregation was a young Jewish man who happened in on the liturgy that day. Later in the sacristy he protested that the celebrant had disparaged his people, that he had implied that the Jews were spiritually dead. We tried to explain to him that in the context the words did not carry that meaning. It was a good example of what it means to live in a language tradition where the same word takes on meanings which it would not have in a different tradition or context.

Language, then, creates us in some sense. It enables us to relate personally with others. One is related to a person by speaking to him. One remains in relation to him only if he answers. And because one is made up of all the relationships that one has, one is made by language, by bodily, symbolic activity. After all, the speaking word is directed to that in us which makes us persons, to our rational, responsible, deciding center. The word mediates meaning which must be understood, judged, accepted or rejected in a free decision. All this is performed by men and women as persons. We are asked to listen but we are free to decline. In either case one sets up new relationships. When someone pursues my friendship actively I can either respond positively or with indifference. In either case I have disposed myself to reality in a new way: in one case I have the new relationship of loving friendship and in the other the lack of this relationship, or something worse such as a relationship of enmity.

When this speaking causes confusion in the listener, when it demands change, when it sets up new relationships, it is called a language-event. This is what Jesus did, especially in the parables. He invited people to share in bold alternatives. For those who accepted this new language, there was a new community. The word, event, is a happy one in this case because it refers to something that affects the whole person and not just the intellectual and verbal part of his being.

Not all language, of course, is eventful. Language is event when as in the case of Jesus referring to God as his Father, it touches the deepest dimension of people's lives. And when this was the case with those who heard Jesus, they entered into a new community, a community that could only stay alive if that language continued to be eventful for them and for others as it originally was. When we call God our loving Father, we have a language-event because it places us in a situation which is different from those who do not call God such. He who hears the word, Father, applied to God cannot do otherwise than decide whether or not he wishes to have this new relationship. He either accepts or rejects it. If he accepts, then he enters into a new community that forms around this word and assents to the relationships implied. This new community shares a language which then becomes his language and his way of relating to others who use the same language and which thus creates a new world in which he lives. This is not the case where the spoken word does not set up new relationships and so is not a language-event or proclamation. For instance, if I tell you that I am wearing nylon underwear, that would not be a proclamation since it does not demand any decision from you. It is not a question of you either rejecting or accepting that fact. I am merely giving information. Proclamation, rather, is that kind of communication that creates reality for the hearer. That means that it gives alternatives, demands decision and requires response. And depending on how people respond to that language-event, their lives will be different in terms of new relationships.

"I love you" is an obvious example of proclamation. My life is different because of the people I love and who love me. Our realities are different because of the relationships. Saying "I love you" makes a difference regarding these relationships. Making the love explicit moves them out of the neutral area. A decision is demanded that makes the relationships different. They become more inevitable, more definitive, more committed. In that sense, an expression of love is not *merely* a celebration of something already present. In the proclamation itself we are actually going beyond the love present in the relationship up to that time.

What does all this mean for liturgy and liturgical planning? It means that liturgy is basically a language, but a language which is more than mere words. Liturgy is a language-event and because it is that, one can affirm that liturgical worship is primarily a situation of proclamation and response. This primordial and unchanging structure of the liturgy must be respected in the process of liturgical planning. Following are certain basic statements which represent in summary form a theology of the liturgy as proclamation.

1. The purpose of God and the person is that there be a union of the two, that there be a sharing of God's creative love with the person and that he become part of the reality of God by means of response. This presupposes the mutual presence of God and the person to each other. In other words, the relationship between God and the person is one of dialog.

2. In this dialog God speaks first; the fundamental attitude of the

person is that of listening. God becomes present in his speaking. Our experience of God is one of communication. God becomes personally and humanly present to us in language.

3. To share in someone's life even through communication, one must be adequately present. God is adequately present to us in Jesus Christ. That is why Jesus is the Word of God, or God's language. Jesus doesn't say everything about God, but he says enough to bring about the sharing, the union without excessive difficulty. In that sense God is adequately present in him.

4. The Word of God has been definitively proclaimed by God. We need but recall it. Our recall is done in language since language answers language. Our response is liturgy. Liturgy is, then, the common language of God and his people. When God speaks to us his Word which is Jesus Christ, we have liturgy in the form of the gospel and the sacraments. When the Christian community responds to God in praise and thanksgiving, we have the language of liturgy. But the liturgical dynamic is not simply one of God's proclamation to us and our response back to him. Christ is seen as the subject of the liturgy rather than the object of worship. In the liturgy Christ is the chief liturgist offering worship to the Father to which we are joined by him. Thus, we can say that in liturgical worship Christ is God's most adequate response. Moreover, since God is in Christ, Jesus becomes God's best answer to his own call and at the same time Christ is the community's fullest proclamation of itself.

5. Liturgy, then, is a situation of proclamation and response. God's proclamation of love to those who believe in his Son constitutes the Body of Christ. The Church is created when the Word is received in faith. The proclamation of the Word of God by the worshipping people also constitutes the Church. In the liturgy both Christ and community proclaim and respond. This proclamation and response structure must find many levels of expression in the liturgical assembly.

6. As the community's proclamation, Christian liturgy is the articulation and intensification of the presence of God and in particular in terms of the Paschal Mystery of Christ: the death, resurrection and exaltation of Jesus. Liturgy is the permanent proclamation of the Paschal Mystery which constitutes and reflects the Church. The liturgical assembly is the most explicit expression and manifestation of the Christian life because it lights up what is going on in the rest of Christian living.

But God is not only present in the liturgy, but wherever people respond to the deepest impulses of nature, wherever they are brought out of isolation to speak a common language. The difference with liturgy is that in the liturgical assembly we can *name* him who brings us out of silence into existence and call him Father.

7. Although liturgy is proclamation, that is, a kind of communication that creates reality for the hearer because it gives alternatives, demands decisions, requires response, makes new relationships and so is a language-event, this does not mean that there must be a new explicit proclamation and response in every liturgy in which one is participating. Most of the real proclamations of God in our lives probably happen outside of liturgy, on occasions when we are confronted with reality in such a way that we are required to be decisive. One thinks for example of the challenging people with whom one works and the various opportunities for growth that happen along each day. But what the liturgy does in relation to those moments of proclamation in our lives is to both affirm and remember the past ones and to anticipate those that will come. Liturgical worship commemorates the past proclamations of God in human living as well as makes one sensitive to those that will enter at some future time. We first encounter the grace of God in human living. In the liturgy this grace is celebrated Liturgy is an explication of God summoning us at the very center of our lives where we discern God's presence and his call to us to create our future.

In conclusion I can only reiterate what I had said in the beginning. The best liturgical adaptation and planning takes place in the context of an adequate liturgical theology. I have tried to indicate the general outlines of a liturgical theology that can serve this purpose. Only with this kind of a theoretical foundation can liturgical planning achieve its final end, namely, that the liturgy be the proclamation of the Body of Christ in our own time.

The following chart is an attempt to concretize the theology of liturgy as proclamation just articulated. While the application is limited to the liturgy of the mass, the principle that all liturgy is structured according to a proclamation/response pattern is valid for all services of worship. Close examination of the chart will show that not all elements of the present normative Roman Rite fit well into this proclamation/response pattern. It is my conviction that this in no way challenges my point that the unchanging structure of all liturgy is proclamation/response. My opinion is that where there is a sense of artificiality in the application of this principle or obvious conflict between the structure of the Roman Rite and this structural principle, the fault lies with the rite. We do not have a perfect liturgy of the Eucharist in the Roman Church. There are still elements in the rite which are misplaced or which should be eliminated entirely. One obvious example is that of the so-called penitential rite which as a unit is really a response. But to what is it a response? There is no preceding proclamation. This rite would better be placed after the reading of the Word of God. Despite these limitations, however, I feel that this chart is a helpful guideline for liturgical planning and a concrete reflection of the liturgical theology developed in this article.

LITURGY AS PROCLAMATION

P & R

LITURGY OF WORD	LITURGY OF EUCHARIST
P	**R**

LITURGY OF WORD (P)

Entrance Song ----------------------------R
Greeting ---------------------------------- P
Amen ------------------------------------- R
Confession ------------------------------- P
Lord, have mercy ------------------------- R
Glory to God ----------------------------- R
Opening Prayer -------------------------- P
Amen ------------------------------------- R
First Reading ----------------------------- P
Responsorial Psalm ---------------------- R
Second Reading -------------------------- P
Silence ------------------------------------ R
Alleluia/Gospel/Homily ---------------- P
Creed ------------------------------------- R
Universal Prayer ------------------------- R

P: Proclamation
R: Response

LITURGY OF EUCHARIST (R)

Preparation Prayers ----------------------P
Blessed be God forever -------------------R
Prayer over gifts ------------------------ P
Amen ------------------------------------- R
Dialog before Preface -------------- P & R
Preface ----------------------------------- P
Holy Holy Holy --------------------------- R
Eucharistic Prayer ----------------------- P
Eucharistic Acclamation ----------------- R
Great Amen ------------------------------- R
Introduction ------------------------------ P
Lord's Prayer ----------------------------- R
Embolism --------------------------------- P
Doxology --------------------------------- R
Prayer for peace ------------------------- P
Amen ------------------------------------- R
Greeting of peace ------------------------ P
And also with you ------------------------ R
Gesture of peace ------------------------- P
Gesture of response ---------------------- R
Fraction Rite ----------------------------- P
Lamb of God ----------------------------- R
This is the Lamb of God ----------------- P
Lord, I am not worthy -------------------- R
The Body of Christ ----------------------- P
Amen ------------------------------------- R
Communion Song/Silence ---------------- R
Post Communion Prayer ------------------ P
Amen ------------------------------------- R
Greeting ---------------------------------- P
And also with you ------------------------ R
Blessing ---------------------------------- P
Amen ------------------------------------- R
Dismissal --------------------------------- P
Thanks be to God ------------------------ R
Closing Song ----------------------------- R

Notes

1. Some of the ideas in this section have been put forth by Gerard T. Broccolo in his article, "A Theology of Worship," which has been published by:

   Liturgy Training Program
   Archdiocese of Chicago
   5947 North Manton Avenue
   Chicago, Illinois 60646

2. In this section dealing with the idea of liturgy as language-event I am indebted to Gabe Huck who has developed this idea in chapter three of his very helpful, but all too brief, book, *Liturgy Needs Community Needs Liturgy* (New York: Paulist Press, 1973), pp. 44 ff. I have referred to some of his examples because they are so persuasive.

3. pp. 403-405.

4. p. 62.

III
The Planning Process

Good Things Don't Just Happen

Michael E. Moynahan, S.J.

Fr. Moynahan has been active in liturgical drama for several years producing plays for the major feasts of the Church. He has also conducted workshops in celebrational style and communication techniques at The Jesuit School of Theology at Berkeley.

I. The Problem

The scene is a familiar one. It is set in our local parish church. The time is the present. The occasion is our weekly celebration of the Eucharist. After the congregation stumbles through three verses of a song they've never heard before, the celebrant makes his way up the center aisle. Two altar boys precede him bumping into one another in four-four time. They look out of place and their actions simply confirm this. The celebrant, chasuble askew, reaches the presidential chair, picks up the portable microphone and begins scratching it. "Is this thing on?" he asks. "Can you hear me in the back?"

From the beginning the liturgy resembles Shakespeare's *Comedy of Errors* more than a celebration of the Lord's Supper. The celebrant is uneasy, the lectors unprepared, the liturgy is uncommunicative, and the general response of the congregation ranges from mild apathy to complete boredom.

There is another scene, quite different in detail, that is symptomatic of the same illness. In this liturgy we are bombarded with non-stop noise. A tactical squad of former Marine drill instructors run a frenzied congregation through an exhausting sixty minutes of high powered liturgical experience. The celebrant has a comment on everything under the sun. His remarks range from creation, to betrayal of public trust by elected officials, to not being afraid to participate, to the role of Christian as prophet, to the difference between law and spirit, to how nice it is that babies cry at liturgies and let us know they are alive, to the sacramentality of the present moment, to the joy of laughing or clapping our hands in church, to God only knows what's next! Every week, at their liturgical celebrations, celebrant and congregation try to tackle all of salvation history through continuous off-the-cuff remarks by the president of the assembly and a dozen favorite folk songs by the Folk-Rock-Hot-N-Tots.

In the first liturgy very little is going on. In the second, too much is happening. Both are the result of little or poor planning. Very few good things happen by chance at liturgies. It takes serious and careful planning to create celebrations that not only meet the needs of the congregation, but challenge them to grow in the areas we, as Christians, so desperately need to grow.

Distinctions must constantly be made when we talk about liturgical planning. The very words excite distrust and apprehension when they fall on certain ears. And yet the careful planning of liturgies is exactly what is needed in many parishes today.

The impetus for renewed and revitalized planning came from the Second Vatican Council's decree on the liturgy. "Pastors of souls must therefore realize that, when the liturgy is celebrated, more is required than the mere observance of the laws governing valid and licit celebration. It is their duty also to ensure that the faithful take part knowingly, actively and fruitfully," (no. 11). The principal way of ensuring thoughtful and effective participation is through serious liturgical planning.

Too many people stand in the way of liturgical renewal and creative adaptation by hiding behind "the law." They mask ignorance, a lack of imagination, and a fear of any type of change, behind the guise of respect for authority.

Sheer legalism, as Vatican II's document on liturgy would support, doesn't exhibit one ounce of good judgment. Tradition is valuable and important, especially for liturgy. But there is nothing good about a blind devotion to law that cannot distinguish between healthy liturgical adaptation and that which is irresponsible. The first type of adaptation consists of innovation in liturgy which is carefully planned and respectful of tradition. The second is liturgical innovation which disregards the meaningful roots, patterns, and rhythms of people and simply manipulates them.

Too many people, pastors and parishioners, cannot distinguish between these radically different responses to the liturgical needs found in parishes today. They lump all innovation, adaptation and planning of liturgy together, and they condemn all of it as bad.

II. What Is Liturgical Planning?

Something that is hastily thrown together can easily fall apart. We have all sat through dull and uneventful classes in school. They were dead. Nothing was happening. They excited little attention, they imparted little knowledge, and they generated little enthusiasm. As students, we responded to these classes with the same amount of interest that teachers exhibited in preparing them—little, if any.

Liturgies that are hastily thrown together also easily fall apart. There is nothing more common to the average worshipper's experience than a dull, poorly planned liturgy.

Good liturgy demands serious and extensive planning. We cannot simply reduce a truly meaningful liturgical experience to a series of mechanical components, but we can finally recognize and acknowledge the importance of certain fundamentals in any well planned liturgy.

These fundamentals or mechanics range from selection and rehearsal of music, to preparation of readings, to insuring that microphones and other audio-visual equipment are in working order, to the selection of one consistent theme, to the coordination of all readings and prayers, to the comments and other things that support and develop a given theme. It is combining all the parts of a liturgy to provide a unified and organic experience that is the constant task of liturgical planners.

And what is liturgical planning? It is many things. It is many people working together to provide their community with the best possible liturgical experience. It is giving focus to a liturgy. It is selecting a theme and giving our worship a direction. It is coordinating all the elements of a given liturgy—readings, prayers, homily, petitions, music, banners and other aids—to bring out and contribute to the development of that one theme.

Liturgical planning is hard work, and lots of it. Planners are constantly looking for the best way to have the Good News proclaimed. Then they seek suitable and meaningful ways for the community to respond. Planning deals with liturgy as a proclamation/response event. Planners continually search for new and better ways of rendering both liturgical proclamations and responses more intelligible, more meaningful, and, in a word, more human.

III. How Do You Plan Liturgies?

First of all, you must see good liturgy as important. You must be convinced of its necessity and its possibility. If you have been exposed to poor liturgy for any length of time, you are more than likely ready. You might begin by asking your pastor about the possibility of a liturgy committee. He'll probably resist at first, but if you keep insisting on the need for a committee and the serious planning of liturgies, you may not only get his approval, but a good block of his time and help.

Next, you must find competent and qualified people. The priests of the parish should be involved as much as possible, especially since they will be your regular celebrators. They can bring an invaluable theological knowledge and perspective to your planning. It would also be a big boon to have someone who has recently done some extensive study and work in the area of liturgy.

You also have to realize that there are a variety of gifts. There are many liturgical charisms floating around in a parish. The important task is to find them and tap them for creating the best possible celebrations for your parish.

The type of people you look for as liturgical planners are: (1) good organizers who have a feel for and desire to create good liturgical celebrations; (2) people with a flair for selecting and directing a variety of types of congregational music; (3) people with an artist's eye for color and arrangement, as well as practical hands for design and construction; (4) a person who is mechanically competent and who is knowledgeable and creative with audio-visual equipment; and (5) someone with experience in drama or theatre who could rehearse readers so they can be understood, and who could also come up with some interesting possibilities for dramatizing the Word of God.

In addition to a group of permanent planners, you must constantly bring in new people. They will bring with them new talent, new ideas, new perspectives, fresh creativity and imagination. And in this way they will keep you from stagnating, and the liturgies you plan from becoming anemic.

And just what does this group of liturgical planners do? Well, each week they should meet together and decide on a theme for their next liturgy. This group can decide on umbrella themes that cover the main divisions of the liturgical calendar: Advent, Christmas, Lent, Holy Week, Easter, and Pentecost. After choosing an umbrella theme, planners can pick a theme for each particular Sunday that will bring out one of the dimensions of that season. Last year, for instance, I was involved in planning the Lenten liturgical series for the Oakland Cathedral. I was one of eight planners for the five Sundays of Lent. And so we chose "Beatitude People" as our umbrella theme for Lent. On each of the five Sundays we developed one of the beatitudes. We chose five of the eight found in Matthew's gospel: Merciful, Pure of Heart, Poor in Spirit, Peacemakers, and Those Who Mourn. Each particular Sunday theme brought out another dimension of what it means for us as Christians to really be a "Beatitude People."

The theme will usually be based on the readings or a reading for a particular Sunday. It is important for planners to be as concrete as possible when selecting a theme. For example, during the season of Advent we choose the particular theme of "Waiting for the Lord." In working with this particular theme, planners must ask themselves questions like "What does it mean for a Christian to wait?" "Who or what do Christians wait for during Advent?" "How do Christians wait?" Perhaps these and other questions will spark your imagination and ingenuity in creating a celebration that will best communicate the theme of "Christian waiting."

In selecting a particular theme, it is important to avoid generalities like loving, believing, or hoping. These types of themes are too vague, the direction or focus of the liturgy is ambiguous. We must limit ourselves and our theme. Only in this way will our efforts be productive. So, planners must narrow down big Christian themes and zero in on one important aspect; they must be specific and concrete.

Once the theme has been narrowed down, planners should begin the process of concretization. They can begin by discussing the selection of readings which convey or support a specific theme. One reading should always be from scripture and preferably from the gospels. If you use two scriptural readings, have one from the Old Testament and one from the New Testament or one from an epistle and one from a gospel. Try not to overlook the Old Testament. There is a wealth of stories of men and women of God that speak powerfully to our own experience of God and the difficulties we all face in trying to lead a God-centered life.

Oftentimes non-scriptural readings can help bring out or develop a theme found in scripture. Here you can suggest a wealth of available literature: selections from poetry, novels, short stories, essays and plays. The excerpt doesn't have to be long. Ordinarily it should be short and to the point. It should serve to support your theme.

Planners should next explore what symbols and signs we have that can best convey a theme. For instance, how can we express mercy? Do we have any merciful signs or gestures? What about a hand extended in friendship? What about a helping or forgiving hand? The kiss of peace takes on added sign value in such a liturgy. And we must not pass over these signs lightly. We must explore and capitalize on their rich symbolic meaning for us.

The possibilities of music should also be explored by planners. What music would best develop or enhance the theme? Here we should not limit ourselves. There is a wealth of contemporary and traditional music that can beautifully and prayerfully support the theme. If it is listening music (i.e. recorded for a responsorial reflection or communion meditation) it must be easy to listen to. If it is for congregational participation, look for simple melodies and un-complicated lyrics. It should be easily learned and sung.

The planning team must also investigate what visuals will help communicate the theme. A picture is worth a thousand words. This is doubly true in liturgy where economy and simplicity of expression are prerequisites for consistently good celebrations. A picture, banner, or single colored slide can convey a theme more eloquently than a forty minute homily. Visuals don't have to replace the spoken word. But they certainly can balance it and contribute to the brevity, clarity, and impact of any theme.

All of the possibilities for readings, symbolic expressions, music, visuals, etc. should be handled in a general brain storming session. The attention and efforts of the planners should be directed at dis-covering how best to concretize the theme. At this time, each member of the planning team should challenge and activate the creativity and imagination of the other members.

After sharing all ideas, the group must begin to pare down all the suggestions to those which best communicate the theme. They must also take into consideration which ideas are most practical given the important limitations of time, talent and resources.

Once these decisions are made, planners must apply the principle of "Divide and Conquer." Distribute the work load as evenly as pos-sible. Someone can work on the selected music. Another can prepare the design and contents of a program. (Programs can be an invalu-able liturgical aid. They should contain any important directions, the words to all songs to be sung at that liturgy, and any responses the people might not be familiar with.) An artist might have an idea for a banner which will help make the theme come alive. Others can select and work on preparing readings, prayers, and everything else planned to help proclaim that week's Good News.

The next important gathering is a day or so prior to the liturgy. If your weekly Eucharist is Sunday morning, then this may mean Sat-urday evening, or Friday evening to play it safe. At this time you should hold what is known, in acting parlance, as a rehearsal.

This is extremely important if you are going to use slides, a film, a mime or dance during the liturgy. Our old general principle applies here too: good things don't just happen. They take time and effort. Practice makes perfect, or at least it can make for a good liturgical experience. At this practice you can get a good idea about what aspects of the liturgy will work, which need ironing out, and which should be abandoned.

If the meaning of anything you are doing or using for the liturgy is unclear to the group, clean it up, change it, or drop it. It will be no more transparent to the congregation than it is to you—generally less. Symbols, gestures, slides, banners, anything you use in the liturgy to help communicate the theme should be simple, unambiguous and self-explanatory. If they are not, they should not be used. They are obviously not good instruments of communication. They do not enhance the liturgy. Therefore, they can only serve to confuse and distract.

The next critical period is thirty minutes before the liturgy. Make sure everything is in its proper place and works. Check all your equipment prior to the liturgy. Leave yourself enough time for something to go wrong. Try to anticipate disasters, especially mechanical difficulties. If you are using audio-visual equipment, make sure you have auxilliary bulbs or machines in case thunder strikes from nowhere and demolishes your projector's light source.

Despite any contrary impression you may have gathered from all that has gone before, remember that liturgy is, and must remain, a prayer experience of the community. It is a lived experience. It is not, and must never become, simply a performance. But an authentic liturgical prayer experience is not antithetical to careful and concerned preparation of liturgical celebrations. A healthy sense of professionalism should characterize all our efforts. This is simply an indication that we see the importance of liturgy in our lives and take the preparation of it seriously. This used to be called "reverence" and "respect."

Finally, sometime after the liturgy, that afternoon or the following day, the planning team should meet and evaluate just exactly what did and did not happen at the liturgy. They must take many things into account, most importantly the reactions of the people whom they serve.

IV. Some Practical Planning Reminders

1. *Liturgical planning is no joke.* It is a serious business. It demands time—lots of it—attention, interest, enthusiasm, reflection, talent, and every ounce of creativity and imagination you possess.

Good things are happening in some parishes with the liturgy because those in charge see it as important. It is a major priority, and as such is given much time and attention by priests and planners.

2. *It can't be done alone.* It takes two to tango and three, four or more to plan liturgy well. No one can do everything. We are all limited. But when we pool our interest and resources, the possibilities for good liturgy become unlimited.

3. *You need freedom and support.* Pastors and people are going to have to give planners the necessary freedom to innovate in liturgy. This freedom is not synonymous with liturgical housecleaning. Innovation does not mean extermination. The old and traditional do not necessarily have to be thrown out. But new ways must be sought to make all aspects of the liturgy more meaningful.

This means that planners constantly need the freedom and encouragement to continually make the signs and symbols of liturgy more clear and transparent to the worshipping community. And this, in turn, demands an understanding of what is happening in liturgy, and the ability to communicate this in the best possible way.

Personal care, concern, and sensitivity to the needs and limitations of a given community must mark the efforts of liturgical planners. And when their efforts are motivated in this way, their work should be met with trust and support.

4. *You don't get somethin' for nothin'.* Good liturgy demands an investment by planners. It is not only an investment of time, talent, energy and enthusiasm, but of dollars and cents. So, liturgy demands a budget. Programs, banners, flowers, decorations, music, musicians, films, slides, etc. all cost money. But when the result is good liturgy, it is well worth the investment.

Planners should approach the work of creating celebrations seriously. They should not treat it like a hobby. The demands on a planner's time are consuming. Priests receive a salary, and so should competent, serious planners. Choir directors, liturgy planners and co-ordinators should be reimbursed in proportion to their qualifications and the amount of time expended by them in creating weekly celebrations.

5. *Beat the bushes.* You don't have to look very far for a wealth of talent and creativity. It lies untapped right within the parish boundaries. Uncover some of those musicians, singers, artists and actors in your parish. Get them involved and make liturgical planning and celebration a real community experience.

There are all sorts of professional talent, college and high school imagination and creativity, and even good old familial common sense, that could really enrich our liturgical celebrations. And how do we tap all of this latent talent? "Seek and you shall find. Ask and you will receive. Knock and it will be opened to you."

6. *Continue the quest.* A liturgy committee's job is not just limited to planning good celebrations. They can dry up fast! Planners are in constant need of education and renewal. They must be prayerful, reflective people who keep abreast of liturgical developments every-

where. They must keep their eyes open and their ears to the ground constantly looking for new and better ways of helping the Word become flesh. In this way they will create liturgies that help us celebrate the presence of the Risen Lord as a community.

7. *Constantly and critically evaluate.* Planners can't work in a vacuum. They also don't live on Olympus. They are usually gifted people, but by no means incapable of error, mistaken judgment, or bad taste with regard to a given liturgy. Planners are not islands unto themselves. They must not isolate themselves from the feelings, experiences and reactions of their communities. They need all of these things in order for their liturgies to be an authentic expression of their community.

Constant evaluation, therefore, must take place. There should be some sort of organized reflection or evaluation after every liturgy. It should be part of the rhythm of a liturgical planner's week. This evaluation must be serious, critical and balanced. What was good about the liturgy? What was bad about the liturgy? What could have been improved? Was the liturgy a prayerful experience? Was it reflective of the community's experience? Was it directed to the people? Did it go over their heads? Did we underestimate where they were? Was an atmosphere of reverence communicated and maintained throughout the liturgy? Was the community nourished by this liturgy? Were they challenged? Was the liturgy an adequate expression of this community's desire and effort to become more a people of God? Did this liturgy artiuclate and celebrate what is going on the rest of the week for this community? These are just some of the many questions planners can and must ask themselves. They must regularly evaluate their efforts to serve the people of God in creating genuine liturgical celebrations.

8. *Remember creation wasn't built in a day!* From the beginning, planners must be realistic, generous and very patient. Start out slowly. Carefully lead the people along. Your first liturgy doesn't have to hit them over the head with a glimpse of the Parousia. You can build to that. Remember that priests, people, and planners are all in this together. Therefore they must all work hand in hand. And it is always helpful in planning that the right hand knows what the left is doing.

Let consideration and cooperation characterize your work. The efforts and hard work of all will be rewarded, in the end, with good liturgy that not only witnesses to but builds up the unity of the worshipping community. It is in this way that we can best praise God in word and deed with our whole being. But this all takes time and much hard work. For after all, good things don't just happen.

Liturgical Planning

John P. Mossi, S.J.

Of late, Eagle Scout Snoopy has been hopelessly lost in the deep woods. He has been caught 'unprepared' to cope adequately with the forest and its environs. Snoopy's predicament is not unlike the experience of liturgical planners. The task seems overwhelming at times. We don't even know where to begin. We can panic as Snoopy does or we can take out our liturgical roadmap and trusty compass to help establish a few coordinates. My colleague, Michael Moynahan, S.J., in his article "Good Things Don't Just Happen" indicates some of the necessary coordinates that help us get out of the liturgical woods. This article offers some complementary practical aids for the planning of thematic liturgies.

Liturgy's Got Rhythm

Try to imagine a melody having a two-note range with all notes receiving the same amount of interpretation and time value. Such a score would be lifeless, flat, and monotonous. Yet how many liturgies come across in this same dull and unimaginative manner? The lack of dynamic movement in the liturgy stems from the failure to properly understand the structure of the new liturgy. Like other art forms, the liturgy possesses its own natural rhythm, its own liturgical cadence. It has its peak moments of primary importance (e.g. the proclamation of the Eucharistic Prayer), and its times for subsequent response, sung meditation, or silence (e.g. the Responsorial Psalm is a sung reply to the First Reading). In effect, the liturgy is punctuated with proclamation/response situations. These proclamation periods and response periods are positioned so that we aren't bombarded with an overdose of strong liturgical statements or lulled to sleep by an absence of variety.

The rhythm of the liturgy rests on the liturgical principle of proclamation/response. Those elements in the liturgy which are of chief importance receive the greatest stress and emphasis. They are proclaimed with care, meaning, and increased intensity. Those parts of the liturgy of secondary importance receive less attention and fewer embellishments. Adhering to the principle of proclamation/response, emphasis/reply, stress/meditation, will underscore the natural dynamic present in the liturgy's structure. It guarantees that the primary elements of a liturgy are correctly emphasized.

Unfortunately, we have too often experienced celebrations in which the Preparation of the Gifts overpowered the Eucharistic Prayer. It is all too common in parochial liturgies that the time and amount of musical stress given to the Penitential Rite and the Glory to God makes the important Liturgy of the Word seem anticlimatic. In many parishes the proclamation of the Breaking of the Bread is minimally ritualized and celebrated. Not only is the Breaking of the Bread one of the four major eucharistic actions of the Mass, it is the sign of the community's reconciliation and unity. Such disregard of the liturgy's natural cadence serves only to confuse and diminish its communication of word, action, and sign.

What is the proper interpretation of the new liturgy's rhythm? The liturgical cadence chart (Diagram #1, p. 78) indicates parts of the Mass which are of major and minor importance. The chart indicates those sections of the liturgy which are to receive greater emphasis by a rise in its cadence line. Notice how the beginning of Mass builds to the proclamation of the Gospel of the Lord. In the Liturgy of the Eucharist, the Eucharistic Prayer, the Breaking of the Bread and Communion are of major importance. These are the parts of the Mass which should be stressed to enhance the celebration.

Preparing the Theme

It is now over ten years after the implementation of the *Constitution on the Sacred Liturgy* and the many directives that flow from its spirit. In light of these guidelines, there is a definite need for all parishes to begin taking seriously the job of planning liturgies. Contrary to the thrusts of Vatican II, there are still many parishes which do not celebrate Sunday with thematically planned liturgies. Others use the helter-skelter method of planning, which runs on chance. Perhaps the high level of congregational absenteeism is a subtle rejection of such worship. It is painfully obvious that minimal efforts beget similar responses.

How does a parish liturgy team begin to thematically plan a liturgy? As Fr. Moynahan suggested, by initially praying over the readings of the particular Sunday three to four weeks in advance. When the liturgy team gathers to prepare the theme, each member will be able to share his or her prayerful insights.

The liturgical season of the year will provide the liturgy team with a hint of the celebration's tone. Since the Gospel is the liturgy's most important reading, it always receives the greatest attention.

Next check the First Reading which is thematically related to the Gospel. This First Reading will give more information on how to further delineate the theme. Then consider the Responsorial Psalm, which should be sung if at all possible. It receives its specific meaning from the Gospel and First Reading. So far so good? A problem arises with the second reading during some Sundays of the year. During Advent, Christmas, Lent, Easter, and special feasts, the Second Reading corresponds to the liturgical season. However during the other Sundays, the Second Reading follows its own sequence. So don't be surprised if you find the Second Reading difficult to work with. Its occasional maverick character will more than challenge your creativity.

Qui Cantat, Bis Orat

Once the theme has been selected and tailored to the needs of the worshiping community, the next step is to embellish the theme musically. If the theme is God's great mercy, then songs to Our Lady, the Holy Spirit, or of national origin are out of place. Special musical consideration is also given to the liturgical season. For example, Easter hymns are not only sung at the Vigil and on Easter Sunday but during the whole of the Easter season. Their repetition on the remaining Easter Sunday helps recall the great joy of the resurrection. For a clear explanation of those parts of the liturgy which should be musically stressed, I strongly recommend reading Fr. John Melloh's excellent article "The Four Hymn Mass."

As certain readings and prayers have precedence over other parts of the Mass, so it is with music. Having music at certain times of the liturgy is more important than at other times. For instance, the opening and closing songs are of secondary importance in relation to the Alleluia, Holy, Memorial Acclamation, Great Amen, and Communion Hymn. However, on major feasts, it is appropriate that the opening and closing songs receive added emphasis. The 'splits' in the cadence chart illustrate that these two songs can receive either festive or moderate attention.

The music chart (Diagram #2, p. 79), complementary to the proclamation/response cadence chart, indicates those parts of the liturgy that are of primary musical importance, secondary importance, and those parts which are best recited. Naturally there will be exceptions to the emphases of the chart. These variations should be carefully made by keeping in mind the purpose, importance, and circumstances of the celebration.

Putting It All Together

Once the liturgy team concretizes the theme and enhances it with musical expression, a liturgical roadmap that will put everything together needs to be filled out. With all the options in the new liturgy, a planning worksheet is a very practical safeguard that prevents visual and verbal miscues. We have all probably experienced embarrassing moments in which commentators or cantors have come in at the wrong time or simply not at all. This causes an interruption in the flow of the liturgy. A planning worksheet is a valuable tool that minimizes such liturgical disasters. Copies of the liturgy worksheet should be given to all who are working on the liturgy at least one week ahead of time. This includes the celebrant, lector, commentator, cantor, organist and all others who are involved.

The accompanying liturgy planning worksheet (Diagram #3, pp. 80-83) is a suggested model for preparing your liturgies. It incorporates the recommendations of Fr. Moynahan's article.

Does this all sound like a lot of work? Well, it is. Especially the first time. Be assured that as you continue to develop your own method, the liturgical forest will proportionately reduce its threatening size.

PROCLAMATION/RESPONSE CADENCE CHART

Diagram #1

Liturgy of the Word

Liturgy of the Eucharist

Entrance Song
Greeting
Penitential Rite
Glory to God
Opening Prayer
First Reading
Responsorial Psalm
Second Reading
Interlude/silence
Alleluia
Gospel
Homily
Profession of Faith
General Intercessions

Presentation of Gifts
Prayer over Gifts
Eucharistic Prayer
Great Amen
Lord's Prayer
Greeting of Peace
Breaking of the Bread
Communion
Thanksgiving
Concluding Prayer
Dismissal
Closing Song

MUSIC CHART
Diagram # 2

	Primary Importance	Secondary Importance	Preferably Recited
Introductory Rite			
Entrance Song		●	
Lord, Have Mercy			●
Glory to God			●
(major feasts)		●	
Opening Prayer			●
Liturgy of the Word			
Responsorial Psalm	●		
(Second Reading)			
Interlude/silence		●	
Alleluia	●		
(Gospel)			
Profession of Faith			●
Intercessory Prayers			●
Liturgy of the Eucharist			
Song at the Preparation of Gifts/interlude		●	
Eicharistic prayer (proclaimed or sung in full or in part)			
Holy	●		
Memorial Acclamation	●		
Great Amen	●		
Communion Rite			
Lord's Prayer		●	
Song at the Greeting of Peace		●	
Breaking of Bread Song		●	
Communion Song	●		
Thanksgiving		●	
Concluding Prayer			●
Closing Song		●	

This Proclamation/Response Cadence Chart and Music Chart are diagrams originating from the lectures of James L. Empereur, S.J.

LITURGY PLANNING WORKSHEET
Diagram #3

Date: _____ Season: _____

Sunday/Feast: _____

Umbrella theme: _____

Specific theme: _____

Liturgy team: _____

Celebrant: _____

Deacon: _____

Communion ministers: _____

Lector: _____

Commentator: _____

Cantor: _____

Eucharistic bread made by: _____

Presentation of gifts: _____

Visuals:
Vestment _____

Drama:
Interpretative reading _____

by _____

Mime _____

by _____

Dance _____

by _____

Dramatic acting of reading _____

by _____

at what part of liturgy _____

Special reading _____

when _____

The Liturgy of the Word

Entrance:
instrumental _____

Processional cross _____

Banner _____

in procession: ☐ yes ☐ no

Antependium _____

Lectern decoration _____

Program design _____

Flowers _____

Slides: _____

Film _____

Other _____

Audio-visual equipment:
overhead projector _____

slide projector _____

movie projector _____

tape recorder _____

operated by: _____

song _____

procession _____

sprinkling _____

Introduction of theme: _____

Penitential Rite: ☐ (1) ☐ (2) ☐ (3) ☐ other

Glory to God: ☐ recite ☐ sung ☐ omit

Introduction to First Reading: _____

First Reading _____

read by _____

Responsorial Psalm: _____

Sung _____

recited with music _____

(continued on page 82)

Introduction to Second Reading: _____

_____

Second Reading _____

read by _____

Alleluia: _____

Gospel procession _____

candles _____

incense _____

Gospel: _____

proclaimed by _____

Homily: _____

Profession of Faith: _____

special form _____

omit _____

Doxology: _____ sung _____ recite _____

Great Amen: _____ sung _____ recite _____

Lord's Prayer _____ recite _____ sung _____

Doxology _____ recite _____ sung _____

Breaking of the Bread
special reading: _____ (1) I Cor. 10:16-17 _____

(2) Acts 2:46 _____

(3) other _____

Lamb of God: _____ recite _____ sung _____

other _____

Communion Song: _____

Thanksgiving:
instrumental _____ song _____

silence _____ slides _____

other _____

Final blessing: _____

General Intercessions: response _____

Prayer over people _____
Recessional:

The Liturgy of the Eucharist

Presentation of Gifts:

instrumental _____

silence _____

song _____

Preface: _____ sung _____ recite _____

Holy: _____ sung _____ recite _____

Eucharistic
Prayer: ☐(1) ☐(2) ☐(3) ☐(4) ☐ other

Memorial
acclamation: ☐(a) ☐(b) ☐(c) ☐(d)

sung _____ recite _____

solemn _____

instrumental _____

song _____

Liturgy and People Power

Rev. Al Hanzal

*Father Hanzal is associate pastor at the Church of Christ
the King in Minneapolis, Minnesota. He has a liturgy degree from Notre Dame and has been director of the Minneapolis-St. Paul Liturgy Office.*

Most Christian celebrations of liturgy suffer the common syndrome of modern living—a lack of people power. Congregations feel
about liturgy the way they feel about government, educational systems, the economy—their decisions or involvement make little difference in the final outcome. Society has made attempts to meet this
lack of power. Education has become more student-centered; con-
sumer groups have made real inputs on corporations; the political
parties are reforming themselves to have all people share in the process of power. The church, too, has made efforts by calling for full,
active participation in the liturgy.

When we move out of a vacuum into the power of people's participation, there can be a natural overreaction. How many parishes in
their eagerness to be with the spirit of the times have simply turned
the liturgy over to a committee of people and told them, "the liturgy
is your work"? Then months later, when little has been done and
many are disillusioned, the experiment is called off. It is declared a
disaster because "people are not ready for such responsibilities."

The great mistake is to expect more of people than they can
comfortably and responsibly give. The ordinary members of a congregation are not competent musicians, they are not expert theologians,
scripture scholars or liturgists. They are Christians who can give a
feeling for what they are experiencing in liturgies and give an honest
reaction to the experience of meeting God's word and sacrament in
their lives. Therein lies their power.

In the fall of 1971, we hesitantly started a contemporary Mass at
Christ the King Church in Minneapolis, Minnesota. The parish is
middle-class, traditional, a semi-suburban mixture of 1500 families.
It has the lines of division most parishes contain between old and new
Catholics, liberals and conservatives. The contemporary Mass was

held in a chapel-church with a 500-600 seating capacity. Later that same year, we found the need to start a second contemporary Mass to handle the overflowing congregation. This fall we face the decision of adding still another. The success of our experience has a number of ingredients: priests who are good celebrants, flexibility, scheduling, two music groups and planning sessions.

It is this last element that has carried the force of the liturgy over the past two years. It is a style of planning that allows genuine people's power. It is combined with the simplicity needed to work with volunteer music groups and busy parish priest schedules.

Scheduling

Every week, the same set time is used for the planning session. This prevents all kinds of unnecessary phone calls coordinating people's schedules. Secretaries, lectors, music people, priests, all know and respect this set time. It is not uncommon for parishioners to also know Tuesday night as "the liturgy planning night."

Lectors

Lectors at the contemporary Masses know the Tuesday night planning session is part of their responsibility as a contemporary lector. Their involvement in the planning sessions gives them the added advantage of having a real feel for what the readings are trying to communicate on Sunday.

Music

One person from the music group participates in the Tuesday night meetings. The theme, tone and music suggestions are taken by this person back to the music group. The group meets later in the week by themselves to put the music together and practice for Sunday. This has a number of advantages: it doesn't make extra meetings for all the music people, a process that can kill volunteer people; it gives them an opportunity to do a final reaction to the music according to their repertoire and competence; it avoids the pitfall of a committee trying to reach consensus on each individual song.

We have an added advantage of two different contemporary music groups. One group plays at both Masses on a given Sunday and then has a week off. This allows two different styles of music, a freshness of not being "on the line" every week, and the opportunity, on the off weeks, for music people to learn from being a part of the congregation. Both groups have found such an approach enriching and stimulating to their growth as music groups.

Celebrants

The three priests in the parish, a pastor and two associates, take turns at the contemporary Mass, and thus create three different styles of celebration. This prevents the parish division that sometimes develops between the young priest doing his "thing" at the contemporary Mass while the pastor takes care of the traditional people. The priest schedule of Sunday Masses is printed in the bulletin the week before. Since many people enjoy following a particular priest at whatever Mass he celebrates, there is a constant flow of always new people at the contemporary Mass. And the parish as a whole feels good about the variety of styles.

Coordinator

One person needs to take the responsibility for contacting families, couples or individuals for the planning sessions. Our religious educator assumes the job, but it could easily be someone else interested in the contemporary liturgy. There are a number of ways of contacting: If there is to be a first communion, baptism or other event celebrated at a contemporary Mass, the people involved are automatically invited to the Tuesday night planning session. The religious educator will often notice those who come frequently to the contemporary Mass, and invites them to a planning session. The priests also have the habit of asking people to plan some Tuesday evening whenever they indicate their enjoyment with the contemporary Mass. A file of names of people interested is kept and it usually takes about a half-hour of calling to set up a month's schedule of those coming in to plan. The people involved are sent copies of the Scripture readings for that particular Sunday and invited to reflect upon them before the meeting.

Planning Session

At a typical contemporary Mass session, the following people are included: the celebrant of the Masses, one person from the music group, the lector for the Mass, one or two families or couples. The meetings are held informally at the rectory.

In the first part of the meeting, the celebrant invites people to give their negative and positive reactions to what has been happening at the contemporary Masses. This grassroots input is vital to making the liturgy responsive to people. Many helpful suggestions have come to the priests, the music people, the lectors, from the people who are the worshipping community. Quite often, people share their deeper feelings about church, the parish or their own way of praying.

The second part focuses on a discussion of the scripture readings. Again, we start with people's honest reactions to what the readings are saying to them and their lives. This is often the most fruitful part of the evening. At times, a given theme for the Sunday develops quickly; at other times it takes far more discussion to reach a concensus on what the readings are saying to people.

Once the theme has been decided, we begin to discuss how we want to express it in prayers, readings, music and action on Sunday. At times another reading is chosen which more clearly expresses the theme. Parts of the service are discussed, opening greetings, penance services, creeds, prayer of the faithful (spontaneous or written), greeting of peace (silence, used at beginning of Mass as form of introduction, prayer form), communion reflections. These parts are judged according to the theme, the tone of the particular celebration, and what is being expressed in the liturgy of the day.

Some discussion is held about the music. Songs are suggested to the music people. Parts of the Mass such as acclamations, Amens and Our Fathers are again determined according to the theme and tone. In these common parts, we have built up a variety of music versions. For example, five different sung versions of the Lord's Prayer. The couple or family may have a favorite version and so give this kind of input into the music. With our suggestions, the theme and tone of the liturgy, the music group meets later to put together a final form.

Finally, the couple planning the liturgy is asked to prepare, before Sunday, a written introduction of the liturgy's theme, working from the ideas of the evening discussion. Some of our most creative thoughts have come in these introductions. The planning couple or family also become part of the offertory procession for the Mass they have planned.

Since we began, two years, almost 200 families or couples have planned the liturgy. They have undergone the liturgical learning involved in the planning process. They have enriched our liturgies and our priests. Those same people are back in the congregation with a different feeling. They know their ideas, their insights into Christianity, do make a difference to the worship of our church. They have a sense of their own power.

To Proclaim His Word

Br. Robert Christian, O.P.

Br. Robert Christian is the past director of St. Albert's Lector Training Program for the Diocese of Oakland. He is now engaged in graduate studies in Sacramental Theology at the Graduate Theological Union, Berkeley.

Since the reformation of the liturgy after the Second Vatican Council, many pastors have succeeded in bringing lay readers into the sanctuary. But if the weekly experiences of most congregations is the standard, they have failed to tell him what to do behind the lectern. Thus, the greater participation of one of the faithful—the lector—is facilitated at the expense of the rest of the worshipping community. For all too often the lector, with the best of intentions, is only reading for himself. Usually this is obvious to everyone except the lector. However, relatively few laity who wish that "something could be done" are willing to volunteer their own talents; and pastors are only too cognizant of this situation. Thus the Word of God, a vital, communicable message of the utmost importance, suffers an agonizing, incomprehensible death. Who cares? More to the point, who can be made to care?

Four years of experimentation with a lector-training program have produced a format which has succeeded in providing parishes with men and women who can communicate the Word of God with dignity, intelligence, and enthusiasm. The key is a balance of emphasis between the medium—vocal skills—and the message. If sacred reading were not something special, a Toastmaster's course or any training in technique would suffice. But because the *what* of Scriptural reading is intimately bound up with the *how* of delivery, the training of lectors involves a knowledge of certain Scriptural themes, liturgical theology, and history, as well as voice projection, inflection, enunciation, pronunciation, etc. If the lector does not know what he is saying, he will not know how to say it. With so many factors to be considered it is clear that a successful program will require careful planning and coordination. For every eight students there should be at least one speech or voice teacher who can give each the individual attention he needs and who can monitor his progress for the duration of the course. Speakers competent in the *what*—the various fields related to the textual material—should be invited to address the participants. The financial burden should be shouldered by the parish or parishes involved, not by the individual registrant.

Obviously, someone planning a lector training program can expect to work hardest before the program actually begins. Once it is under way, it takes care of itself.

What steps, then, should someone interested in improving the quality of sacred reading take?

1. Both teachers and lectors should meet for 8 weeks, with one session per week. Week nights are generally preferred to Saturday mornings. Therefore, the first step is to find a week night that is convenient (i.e., not interrupted by holidays, vacation seasons, elections, etc.) for eight consecutive weeks. January, February and March are relatively uncluttered months.

2. Determine the format of the meetings. To give the lectors a sense of the distinctiveness of their role, the following schedule might be adopted. Each meeting would begin with a one-half hour presentation on some aspect of the liturgy or the Scriptures delivered by a qualified guest speaker. This would be followed by fifteen minutes for questions and discussion and another fifteen minutes for coffee. Inspired by the lecture and fortified by the refreshments, the lectors would then be ready for ninety minutes of technical training. Thus, each session would be two and one-half hours long, but would be broken up into different parts so that the participants, already tired after a day at work, would not be unduly wearied by a single, prolonged meeting.

3. Determine the costs. Professional speech teachers should be paid an adquate salary. Their ninety minute appearance once a week represents a substantial investment of their time. But the preparation of lectors not simply to read well, but to communicate and proclaim the Word of God in a liturgical setting is worth the expense. The costs of advertising, mailing, refreshments, and certificates of completion should be included.

4. Publicize the program at least six weeks in advance. Mail a flyer to local Catholic parishes and to Protestant churches with a liturgical tradition. Notify the bishop of your plans and invite him to meet your group, perhaps on the final evening. The greatest response seems to come from advertisements in Catholic papers and news releases in the secular press. And should the program become an annual offering, alumni should be informed to spread the news by word of mouth.

5. Decide what topics, besides technical training, the course will include. Certainly some broad addresses on liturgical history, symbolic communication, and the role of the laity in the new liturgy could be included. Many scriptural themes might also be helpful, e.g., suffering in the scriptures, literary genres and oral traditions in the Old and New Testaments, revelation, inspiration, salvation and St. Paul, praying the scriptures, etc.

6. Hire personnel. This can be tricky when done before knowing your enrollment, but if you have an enrollment or payment cut-off date (e.g., ten days before classes begin), people who have tentatively committed themselves to teach can be informed definitely whether or not they will be needed. Good starting places to search for personnel are Catholic high school speech departments and seminary or scholasticate homiletics departments. Seminaries will also be able to supply, at little or no cost, guest speakers for the *what* of lector training.

7. Arrange for classrooms, blackboards, tapes, microphones, and church practices.

8. Divide the participants into groups equal in size but of both sexes and various age groups.

When these points are taken care of, only minimal supervision and some weekly coffee-making will be needed for the duration of the course. When the program has finished, have the lectors evaluate their experience so that the next session will be even better.

This is a lot of work, much of it drudgery, but the Word of God demands no less—or did you miss that at last Sunday's Mass?

IV
The Environment
for
Worship

Worship Space and Design

James Notebaart

The Reverend James Notebaart has a master's degree in sacramental theology from St. Paul's Seminary in Minnesota. He has studied the arts at Catholic University of America and is now studying architectural and environmental design at the Minneapolis College of Art and Design and the University of Minnesota. Fr. Notebaart is interested in ritual and the environment of ritual.

How many times have you gone into a church for a special event and found the church just like it always is except for two bouquets of flowers? This is a bleak testimony to our inability to decorate a space outside of certain narrow structures. We often don't let our minds wander to new ways of visually saying celebration, new ways of saying something Christian is happening here. Part of the problem is a confusion about how we, the American melting pot, can put core truths into ritual. This is a failure or inability to understand our lives in ritual terms. And this problem is not easily solved. However, there are less serious problems that are easily solved. One reason for the sameness in our churches is that we get caught up in what is easiest to do. We find it immensely easier to order two bouquets of flowers than to plan something that will take time to construct. Oftentimes we become frightened by creativity, and we feel we just don't have what it takes to be creative. We do this because we overestimate the creative person. Creativity is largely a matter of good taste. It is largely a matter of understanding the restrictions and advantages of the place we want to decorate.

We shouldn't be frightened of our own creative efforts, yet we should try to observe a few ground rules in our creativity. For creativity really arises out of the definition of the project. If we know our limits, our rules, we will be creative. So, in a way, even with creativity there are limits. We can't do anything and label it creativity, because this might merely be misuse. But just as we shouldn't be frightened by our own creative efforts, we shouldn't become frightened about the rules of design, for they are really there to help us in our creativity.

The following, then, is a presentation of the rules in one small area of creativity: the creative use of the space of worship.

All design is an attempt to create visual order and beauty in the whole of one's experience. To create a design for a particular event, one focuses attention on a theme in such a way that all of one's senses are brought into harmony. To design a space for an event means that everything about that space should be considered. We must consider all the elements, the building, the light, the shape, the color, the theme and its feeling.

The Building

Every church, or hall, or place of liturgy is really quite different; each has its own drawbacks as well as its good points. The whole space, the total volume is the arena of our decoration. It isn't just the sanctuary which is the area of design. When we gather for liturgy, we are all celebrants together and there is a dialogue between what we see and how we respond. The entire space says something to us. The size of the space will often determine what we can do and what experience we can have. We might want to capitalize on the space or limit it. The classical example is President Johnson's daughter's wedding. It was held in the National Shrine in Washington, D.C. The space is immense and there were only four hundred people attending. To *limit* the space the Johnsons had trees brought into the church to cut off the sides visually. This allowed them to have a small wedding and yet use the space well without feeling lost in it.

One can also *capitalize* on the space. Height is a sense used often in liturgy; certain times of the year celebrate height. Easter, for instance, is one of these times. Why not use the vertical thrust of a church to express this. Our church has a thirty-five foot ceiling. Easter gave us the opportunity for a fifteen-foot banner mobile, hung from the ceiling with a ten-foot candle and stand below it. We tried to use the natural height of the room to its own advantage.

One can use the narrowness of space to the advantage of design as well. Intimacy and even oppression, although opposite, are senses of liturgy that really capitalize on smallness and narrowness of space. The sense of gathering within a baptistry in some crowded fashion can work to one's advantage when you relate it to the rest of the space.

We Must Know the Space

Once we have come to understand that the whole space is the arena of our design, we should analyze the space that we have. We must ask ourselves: How can we change the space in order to express the mood of a particular liturgy? The answer comes in our own understanding of the space. The character and feeling of the space will determine what we can do. Some churches have vast expanses of wall space; some are visually complex; some are austere. Some are places of great volume and others are oppressive in their lack of volume. Is your church Victorian Gothic? Is it austere Georgian? Is it German baroque? How does it feel when you are in your church before you do anything to it? How do you want to feel for a particular event?

Every Part Is Part of the Whole

Once we have defined the space, we can change the experience we have in it. But we must remember that our design is an integral thing. We can't change one area without considering how it will affect the whole experience. The whole space, the floor, the ceiling, the walls, the pillars; everything is the ground for design, and all of it is affected by changing any part of the space. If we keep this in mind we will tend to use the space more fully, and our designs will not be concentrated in any one area.

How Do You Want the Space To Function?

The next step in trying to be creative with the worship space is in answer to the questions: What do you want the space to do? Or, what moods do you want to express? Many times the space may work well without changing it in any way or merely by making minor changes such as using more or less lighting for a specific liturgy or for a specific effect. But if you feel that the space can be changed in order to bring out the theme or experience better, then you must find out exactly what you want to say. Do you want the space to bring the people into a closer relationship visually? Do you want the space to be peaceful, quiet, or filled with life? How does a space give the experience of death? The answers to these questions are moods that the space can express.

Is the Event Important Enough to Change the Space?

We know that the way we use design can express a focus, but we must first determine the importance of the event that we are celebrating. We really shouldn't make major visual experiences for events that aren't of major proportions. In the Church, every Sunday is not of the same religious importance. Pentecost Sunday is more festive than the 23rd Sunday after Pentecost. If the event warrants a major visual change such as Easter does, we have to determine how to bring about this change in our church. Maybe because of the character of our church we will not have to do much to express the design. An austere space can be significantly changed merely by a few visual elements. A more complex space really demands more care in bringing about the desired effect without cluttering it beyond recognition.

The Changes We Make Are Not Permanent

Have you ever gone into a church where the same series of banners have been hanging for several years? They have become permanent decorations. This misses the whole point of decorating for an event. Whatever effect a space is going to have for a particular celebration, that effect really shouldn't become part of the space. If the decorations are left, they will continually complicate each succeeding period of decoration. Only a good fire could allow you to start over then. So, at the very beginning, whatever you do, do it and then take it down. This should be part of our thinking from the very moment we start to make plans.

There Is a Proportion to Our Designs

After we know the event we want to celebrate, one of the most important elements in our design is that we proportion the visual experience we want to the space in which we are working. One can never decide on the size for something unless he first has imagined it in the place where it will go. In fact, the whole process of design is one of continually relating what we are thinking to what can be done. It is a process of bringing about what we visualize. We must always visualize our design in the space and in relation to the architecture.

When St. Peter's Church in Rome was dedicated they hung a 70-foot banner in the dome with the papal coat of arms on it. The letters of the various inscriptions around the dome are six feet high. This is an example of proportion to space. An Easter candle that is an inch thick in a hundred-foot-long church will look like a thread from the back of the church. We should ask ourselves: What is the Easter candle supposed to say? And is Resurrection *visually* spindly? Or further, a 25-foot Christmas tree in a 35-foot-high church is better, no doubt, than a six-foot one. An Advent wreath that is 9 feet across might be better than a two-foot one, if the space demands it. Determine the basic thrusts of the church. Is it vertical? Is it horizontal and low? Once we have discovered these things, we must ask ourselves how we want our designs to relate to the basic thrusts of the church. We want to determine a proportion for our church.

Where Should the Visual Elements Be Placed?

Since the whole space is the ground for celebration and we know the proportions in which we are working, we next must ask ourselves where the visual elements should be placed. Maybe the effect that we want can be brought about at the entrance. The people will see it when they first come in and it won't say anything to them until they leave again. This might be a little more subtle than having to face the visual elements throughout the celebration. Maybe the event itself will warrant only a passing mood setter rather than hitting the people with a blunt statement. There are areas of focus within the church; for instance, if we have a visually strong Easter candle, why not place it where it can be used most meaningfully, at the entrance, or in the middle of the church, or near the pulpit, or at the baptistry, or maybe throughout the year in each of these places as the event dictates. Make use of the many places that are part of the space, sometimes one, sometimes another, sometimes many.

Variety

One of the most important factors in the design of a comprehensive decoration program is that variety is a key to experience. But just as there are certain events that are more important than others, I don't think we want to change the whole thing around all the time. In other words, variety is healthy and good, if not essential, but the worshipping community cannot be battered by constant change, so that they never know where they are at. Like the Church's celebrations, there are quiet seasons, the "ordinary Sundays," and there are the festive times. Too much variety can destroy rather than build celebration. We must take into account the community and make decisions of visual changes with great sensitivity, because, ultimately, the visual elements are only aids in the celebration. Nevertheless, variety is important in the decisions we make about the visual experience of the space.

The Elements of Design

Many of the above guidelines have examined how we are to relate to the space of celebration. And they are critical guidelines in using the design elements. The design elements are the components of any design. Listed simply, they are:
— the point,
— the line,
— the form,

— two and three dimensions,
— value (light and dark),
— color,
— texture (surface quality), and
— the plane.

All visual experience is found within these elements and their relationship. To use design is to organize these parts within your own purpose of creating a harmonious whole. We often don't bother to break down design into these elements and we just think "banner." But to demonstrate how helpful it can be, let's just take the concept of line or verticality. A line is grass; it is calligraphy; it is pipes, poles, wires, railways and rainbows. A line is lights at night and beams of light. It is rain from a distance and vines in place, and spider webs. And, lastly, it is a banner. Look how many design elements have been added to "verticality means banners." The Guthrie theater, for its performance of *Becket,* took the design element "line" and the whole set was a working out of this one element. It was a ladder of boards, simply austerely vertical. They were the doors of the cathedral, the chair of the king, and, when light came through them on the floor, they were solemn witnesses to death. It is how they used this concept of line that created the effect. The set never changed. If we want verticality, does it mean banners? What else can you come up with to create a design?

Types of Decorations

Once we know the design elements we can be more creative in finding ways of decorating. But here is a listing of a few elements that are already used and may be able to be used more creatively. The standard decorations are flowers, banners, and candles. These have almost become so standard that they have lost their sense of setting the mood for prayer. Maybe we can use them in a different way. Banners, for instance, don't have to be three feet by six feet. They can be five inches by eight feet. They can be thirty inches by fourteen feet. They can be used by putting them on the wall, by carrying them, by having them stand free in the congregation. They can be grouped in containers casually. They can be hung from the ceiling in tiers. They can be multi-leveled and transparent. And banners can be made not only of burlap, but-silk, wool, plastic, wood and metal as well. A banner is a concept, not a shape or material. It doesn't have to have words and texts on it. It is a mood setter, not another form of "Word." The "word" of the banner is *itself,* hanging, suspended and real, not something you read. It tells us how to feel by letting us feel its mood.

Flowers don't have to be in front of the altar, or they don't have to be in the sanctuary. They can be anywhere. They can be hung; they can be in the midst of people. They can be in their hands. They don't have to be arranged in formal triangles by florists; they can be bunches that children pick, just like they pick them for their mothers.

And candles aren't always in metal holders. They can be in bunches or tall, formal guards at the altar. They can be on branches or stuck into a bowl of sand on the altar. They can be clustered around a focal point for a particular service, a cross, for instance. You can have one candle, you can have thirty. It just depends on what you want to experience.

These are the three standard decorations in churches. The following is a short list of some other items. It is by no means a taxative list. One can use branches quite effectively to express either new life or austerity. Mobiles made of metal or pictures or material or weaving or wicker are possible. Portable kiosks (large chests) that are well designed can become storage and design. They can be walls, towers, picture boards. Photo-murals can be framed and be a focus for many events. And the wealth of all art is the subject here. One really has no limit in design; good taste is the main criterion and the space in which the design is to work is critical.

Style

In choosing how to create a design for your church you must be led to less explicit kinds of statements. For example, Pentecost is not a dove but an experience of the Spirit. Often we have over "doved" our visual experience. We have often over killed our celebrations because we have been too explicit . . . too clear in establishing our experience. And what we have lost is the art and the mystery of the moment and the coalescence of our own faith within the event of the liturgy. Whatever we do about design, it is not meant to say something about the liturgy alone but to become part of the dynamic of the event. Our use of design is the forum for celebrating ourselves in God's eyes.

Consultation

A good rule of thumb in making decisions about the design for a specific liturgy is that it never hurts to consult competent people. Every parish has a good number of people with excellent taste and some who have been trained visually. Do not hesitate to call upon them. It is their value judgments that can pull the design together.

The Liturgical Environment

John P. Mossi, S.J.

The eleventh chapter of Genesis relates the account of the tower of Babel. As the story goes, the ambitious builders sought dimensions beyond their capacities. What was supposed to unite earth with heaven resulted in chaos. The tower became cluttered with confusion and architectural ambiguity.

Unfortunately, the Tower of Babel is alive and well today in many of our houses of worship. Billboard jungles of conflicting images, symbols, and devotional areas impinge on one another's territory manifesting an environmental lack of good taste. By means of some unwritten law, our churches tend to be collectors of all kinds of statues, paintings, and artifacts that would find entry into a wax museum quite difficult. In short, many of our houses of worship are in need of environmental cleaning.

In light of Vatican II and current trends in incarnational theology, a serious and critical look must be given to the contents of our churches. For instance, do the liturgical furnishings, art objects, decor, etc. express who we are, reflect our contemporary society, assist our devotion and prayer, or critique our actions? A harmonious environment can do this and more. It can enhance the religious expression of worship and engage the congregation in more meaningful prayer.

The recent interest in liturgical environment stems from an increased awareness of the dependent relationship that exists between theology—the message, and interior design—the medium. The liturgical environment is the theological statement and mood that the church's interior creates. This expression of theology is found in everything from the design, size, color, positioning of the table of the Lord—the altar, to its appointments. This expression is found in the placement of the pulpit, the arrangement of the congregational seating, the location and contents of stained-glass windows, the length and width of banners, the type of vestments worn, the intensity of light in the sanctuary, and on and on. The list is endless. The intent of the liturgical environment is to create a unifying experience of worship, warmth, fellowship, and prayer.

You might readily object, "What does environment and architec-

100

tural mood have to do with going to church?" Perhaps more than we realize. Our faith and theology is not just confined to the Word of God, the celebrant's homily, or the Great Eucharistic Prayer. The whole of creation praises the Lord. This means that the aesthetically pleasing contours of the church's architectural form, color combinations, artistic ornamentation, and its use of wood, metal, stone, and glass are all hopefully blending to reveal the incarnational beauty of God in the world. Consequently, the total arrangement of the church, from entrance to sanctuary, is constantly speaking to us. In an environmentally balanced church, the environment aids the liturgy and enhances the ritual strivings of celebrant and people. It helps make the liturgy function. The Second Vatican Council states in the *Constitution on the Sacred Liturgy,* in its chapter titled "Sacred Art and Sacred Furnishings":

"When churches are to be built, let great care be taken that they be suitable to the celebration of liturgical services and for the participation of the faithful."

Two basic considerations which come to mind are essential to environmentally implement this Vatican II spirit: *proximity* and *visibility.* They are mutually dependent. The greater the proximity to the celebration, the greater meaning will the liturgical signs and actions convey.

PROXIMITY

In contemporary times, the relocation of the altar facing the congregation theologically states that Christ, represented by the altar, is the center of our lives and worship. The altar facing the people says that the celebration of Mass belongs to the entire worshiping body, not just the priest. We have experienced an environmental change. Reverence, which was at one time expressed by recessing the altar deep into the sanctuary, distant from the people, emerges in its new forms of proximity and transparency.

One possible design that communicates this refocusing of God in our midst is a 180-degree fan-shape church with an adequately large sanctuary projected into the center of the fan. In such an environment not only are the Word of God and the table of the Lord the obvious and proximate heart of the worship, but also the people are immediately present to the celebrant and to one another. A greater sense of community and participation is encouraged by such a structure.

Pre Vatican II Model

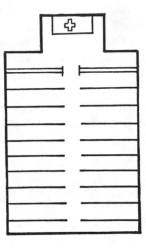

Post Vatican II Model

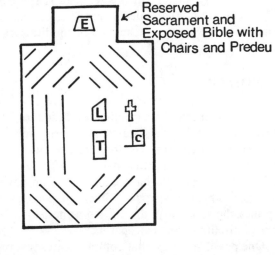

Reserved
Sacrament and
Exposed Bible with
Chairs and Predeu

L Lectern
T Table of the Lord
C Celebrant's Chair
† Cross
E Eucharist
B Baptismal Font

Churches that are long and narrow can easily handle the problem of separation of priest and people by thrusting the sanctuary a few rows into the body of the church. The process would eliminate the altar rail leaving the sanctuary a freer, open, and more inviting space. The seating can be switched to a V-shaped arrangement by diagonally facing the pews toward the center aisle. This permits the congregation to better see and hear their neighboring section.

V-SHAPED REMODELED CHURCH

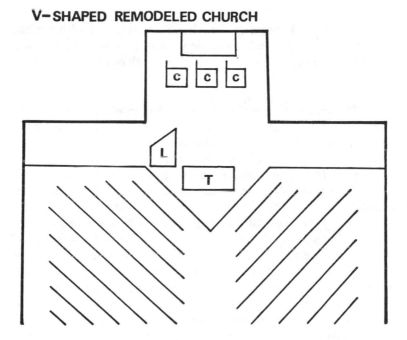

Lighting cannot be overlooked for it is a crucial means of creating focus of attention. In the new sanctuary, the lectern, table of the Lord, and celebrant's chair are of primary importance. These areas require ample lighting. Other parts of the church should remain quietly subdued so as not to become distracting.

The thrusting of the sanctuary into the congregation is a significant step in updating the environment for liturgy. It represents a concrete statement in form and material that the worship of the local community is a central, tangible, and proximate experience.

VISIBILITY

Most of us have looked at beautiful vistas only to find the natural scene interrupted by twenty foot neon signs flashing "EATS" or "RIDE THE GOLDEN FLEET." Their distasteful effect causes one to wonder if a more environmentally respectful form of communication could be employed. Similarly, we must question the environmental settings of our churches. The 1970 General Instruction of the Roman Missal is very explicit about the focal area reserved for liturgy:

> "Images should, however, be placed so as not to distract the faithful from the actual celebration. Also, they should not be too numerous, and there should not be more than one image of the same saint."

The heavenly choir motif that is prevalent in older churches is to be seriously reviewed as to their quality, quantity, and positioning. Statues of Christ, Mary, or the saints, with their respective rows of candles, should not be in or near the sanctuary proper. However, the 1970 General Instruction encourages the positioning of a free standing crucifix near the altar. The crucifix, besides being a low key environmental accent, can also be effectively used for processions.

In general the decor of the church should be contemporary, assisted by selective use of natural materials and simple designs, and free from the overcrowding of furniture and art work. Except for those places of historical or true architectural value, the preservation of highly intricate ornamentation in altar, walls, and ceiling is not in keeping with liturgical trends toward simplicity of expression. The congregation's line of vision should be able to easily center on the lectern, the table of the Lord, and the celebrant. Whatever distracts or visually clogs these primary signs of proclamation and unity is either to be eliminated or significantly reduced in its importance.

Some parishes hedge on any attempt to renovate their houses of worship because of the expected reaction from certain individuals. Hopefully any remodeling will be preceded by adequate preparation and instruction. Many objections quickly disappear when the purpose of liturgical renovation is understood and made clear. The reason for rearranging our churches is really to make our worship environment more traditional; that is, more attuned to the actual worship experience of the early church. Christ the King Church in San Diego, California handled this touchy problem of remodeling while at the

SANCTUARY OF CHRIST THE KING

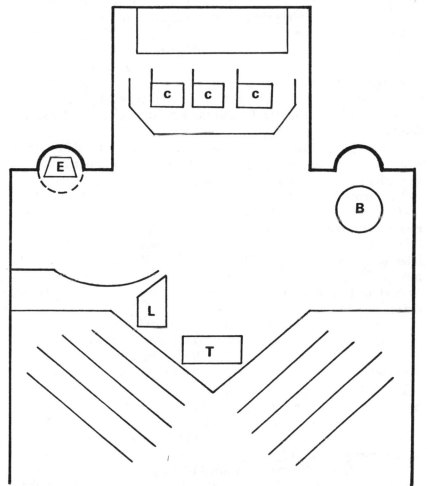

same time satisfying groups with divergent interests. Here is the practical solution they agreed upon: thrust the sanctuary into the congregation and alter the pews to V-position; eliminate the barrier of the
altar rail except for the section in front of Mary's altar and transfer
the tabernacle to Mary's altar; move the statue of Mary to St. Joseph's altar thereby ending our separation of them and eliminate the
other statues surrounding the side altars; relocate the baptismal font
in front of Joseph and Mary and redesign the old baptistry as a saint
grotto. The advantages of such updating are manifold. Word and
Eucharist are in unquestionable prominence, the Blessed Sacrament
is reserved in a more private area of the church which is suitable for
personal devotion, the baptismal font occupies a visual place of importance next to the sanctuary, and the baptistry serves as a special
devotion and prayer room.

Liturgical environment affects much more than just architectural
design and allotment of church space. There are other important considerations. For instance, in designing an altar it is preferable to
make it moveable. A portable altar brings flexibility into the sanctuary area. Depending on the occasion the sanctuary can easily be arranged for large weddings, group baptisms, anointings, as well as offering extra space needed for dramatic presentations of readings,
interpretations of the gospel, liturgical ballet, mime, or creative use of
media, slides, overhead projection, or film. What was once a very restricted area of worship now opens itself up to accommodate a variety of special liturgies.

Through strategic employment of a moveable altar, a heightened
awareness and distinction between Word and Eucharist is easily
achieved. During the liturgy of the Word, the lectern receives the
center of importance and prominence. During the preparation of the
gifts, the lectern is moved to one side and the table of the Lord is
brought forward to signify the commencement of the meal liturgy.

Another way that the liturgy of the Word and the Eucharist can
be underscored is through processional candles. These can flank the
lectern during the readings and homily, then be repositioned on either
side of the altar during the preparation of the gifts.

As the church should be uncluttered, so should the table of the
Lord convey the same simplicity. The meal action of the Eucharist
and the sign value of the wine and bread is oftentimes obstructed by a
visual blockade of flower arrangements, bulky candle holders, book-
stands, raised prayer cards, and crucifix. These help create a wall between the Eucharist and the people. Only what is of absolute necessity belongs on the table of the Lord; namely, chalice, communion

plate, purificator, and Mass book. In such a way the obvious sign of the bread and wine occupy the visual focus of attention and speak unconfusedly for themselves.

Another way to bring environmental attention to the table of the Lord is through the use of a variety of altar cloths. Different colors,

MOVEABLE LECTERN and TABLE of the LORD

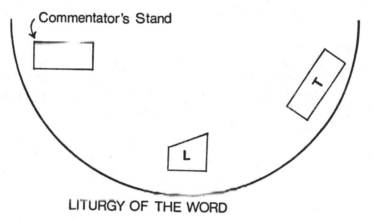

LITURGY OF THE WORD

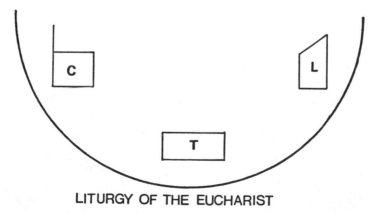

LITURGY OF THE EUCHARIST

shapes, and patterns can effectively be employed to carry the liturgical color of the season or complement the celebrant's vestments.

Regarding the vessels for the Eucharistic meal, two materials have become increasingly popular: earthenware and glass. The resurgence in homemade crafts has provided some parishes with a variety of creative liturgical chalices, plates, and fixtures. The local community can be a valuable liturgical resource who can contribute their talents and insights thereby adding a new personal meaning to the celebration. Glass is another excellent material to use on the altar, especially since it lends itself to manifesting the sign value of the wine. Just as the sign value of the wine should be visible to all, the sign of the bread should be as obvious. The 1970 General Instruction of the Roman Missal indicates that the bread is to have the actual appearance of bread. The thin wafers presently in use convey a poor sign value of bread and consequently are deficient in their meaning. Their replacement is long overdue.

There are other equally important aspects of worship like audibility, music, role of the celebrant, liturgical movement, color and design on which space prevents further comment. Hopefully this article has provided some creative and practical suggestions that will help parish liturgies become more unifying, expressive, and prayerful, and that will enable the worship experience to be more proximate and visible. The result should be a worship experience that takes into its scope the total liturgical environment—everything from the arrangement of furnishings to the hospitality expressed by the congregation and ministers.

The Liturgical Year

Warren J. Rouse, O.F.M.

*Father Rouse is currently pastor at Holy Family Parish,
Pueblo, Colorado. Father is also an active member of the
Federation of Diocesan Liturgical Commissions.*

For a number of centuries—indeed, down to recent decades—
popular devotion and pious books gave the distinct impression of
"play-acting" with regard to the Mass. Architecturally, the crucifix
rather than the altar table was visibly dominant. There was a hushed
silence—not dissimilar to the atmosphere of a funeral home—during
Mass and the priestly chasuble was adorned with a cross. Meditation
books offered such thoughts for reflection (since missals were nonex-
istent).

At the prayers at the foot of the altar, we are to consider Christ
and His apostles in the garden of Gethsemane; at the "Lavabo" the
priest represents Pontius Pilate washing his hands; the reason for consecrating both the bread and the wine is to symbolize the separation
of Christ's body and blood in death.

The descriptive terms employed—while theologically accurate—
were "Sacrifice of the Cross" and "Re-enactment of Calvary," both
of which seemed to indicate that somehow Christ again died symboli-
cally during Mass, with little emphasis on His resurrection. This implicit "play-acting" extended to the other feasts celebrated throughout the year.

What we had unconsciously adopted was a "cyclic" view of time
common to primitive religions, which saw the present moment as
meaningless; only the re-enactment of a primordial event had value.
Mircea Eliade explains: "Reality is acquired solely through repetition
or participation. . . The man of a traditional culture sees himself as
real only to the extent that he ceases to be himself and is satisfied
with imitating and repeating the gestures of another." And in particular: "All sacrifices are performed at the same mythical instant of
the beginning; through the rite, profane time and duration are suspended." For the pagans, the value of the rite was to put them into
contact with the only reality: that of a past event.

But a unique feature of Judaism was a "linear" concept of time: "For the first time we find affirmed and increasingly accepted, the idea that historal events have a value *in themselves,* insofar as they are determined by the will of God. This God of the Jewish people is a personality who ceaselessly intervenes in history, who reveals his will through events. . . The Hebrews were the first to discover the meaning of history as the epiphany of God, and this conception was taken up and amplified by Christianity." *(Cosmos and History)*

When the early Christians gathered for the Eucharist, consequently, they were aware, as Edward Schilleebeckx points out, that "time itself is irreversible. Whatever is historically past cannot now, in any way at all, be made once more actually present, not even by God himself. Whatever has already happened in history is irrevocably past and done. A fact historically past cannot therefore be actualized anew mystically or in the sacrament."

Christ died once and for all on a certain day in a certain year. But what remains is His salvific will for all eternity. Thus the Eucharist is indeed a recalling and the application *here and now* of the redemptive grace. There is a parallel with the Jewish Passover celebration each year: hundreds of years after the Exodus the Jews gathered for this formal meal. The first part of the ceremonial was a recalling of the wonderful deeds of God. But this was followed by the formal eucharist or thanksgiving, in which the head of the family here-and-now definitively said in effect: "The 'yes' our forefathers said to you in the past, O God, we wish to re-affirm for ourselves "today." This was precisely because of their awareness that immersion into the covenant had to be something personal.

Like the Jews, the early Church developed a year's cycle founded on the Easter event and the "little Easter" which was Sunday. This was virtually necessary, as one author explains: "When, after the extraordinary freshness of its origins, the Church had to adapt itself to a longer waiting period; a certain regularity in its prayer-life became necessary in order that this time of waiting might still be one of ceaseless vigilance, and that the remaining span of life upon earth might not be wasted. . . Thus it was that the rhythms of creation were taken into service to help us on our journey to meet the Lord, and the yearly cycle of life on earth was more and more used to enable us to share in the mystery of Christ."

The theological impact of the fully developed liturgical year was described by Pope Pius XII in his encyclical, *Mediator Dei:* "The liturgical year, animated throughout by the devotion of the Church, is no cold and lifeless representation of past events, no mere historical record. It is Christ Himself, living on in His Church, and still pursuing that path of boundless mercy which, 'going about and doing good,' He began to tread during His life on earth. This He did in order that the souls of men might come into contact with His mysteries and, so to speak, live by them." This echoes the thought years before of Columbia Marmion in his still superb book, *Christ in His Mysteries:* "It is true that in their historical, material duration, the mysteries of Christ's terrestrial life are now past; but *their virtue remains,* and the grace which gives us a share therein is always operating."

Recently the liturgical calendar underwent reform at the request of Paul VI who recalled that "with the passage of centuries, the faithful have become accustomed to so many special religious devotions that the principal mysteries of the redemption have lost their proper place. This was due partly to the increased number of vigils, holydays and octaves, partly to the gradual dominance of various seasons over the entire liturgical year."

The purpose of the restoration of the liturgical year and the revision of its norms is none other than to allow the faithful, through their faith, hope and love, to share more deeply in "the whole mystery of Christ as it unfolds throughout the year."

Building the Non-Verbal

John P. Mossi, S.J.

In recent years, we have witnessed a long overdue liturgical housecleaning. The baroque styles so prevalent in church architecture, sacred art, and music, the structure and ceremony of the liturgy have all been streamlined. This needed, theologically informed updating has been both beneficial and detrimental to the quality of our worship experience. We have remodeled our churches, modernized the music, and simplified the Mass. We rightfully focus our maximum attention on the Liturgy of the Word and the Eucharistic Banquet. Yet at the same time, an important worship quality seems lacking: ritual action, the non-verbal, religious movement, sacred dance, call it what you will. This poverty of liturgical beauty, interior soul, or non-verbal involvement should be of no surprise to us because the principal communication medium of the new liturgy is the spoken word. The new liturgy has a built-in tendency to be a verbal overdose, a didactic barrage.

One exasperated parishioner expressed his feelings this way, "Commentators explain the obvious, lectors attempt to digest the readings with summaries that are longer than the scripture texts, celebrants rush through prayers as if on a freeway, even cantors feel they have to remark on the theology of the Mass or repeat the hymn title and page till nausea sets in. I feel like I'm being attacked by words!"

The Non-Verbal

The parishioner's complaint is well worth considering. The new liturgy, now more richly understood due to the use of the vernacular, needs the subtle refinements of the non-verbal to deepen its beauty. Such ritual expression is actually present in the new liturgy, but in too few places has it been effectively utilized. We tend to celebrate under the verbal myth that creedal recitations, clear and distinct ideas, Ciceronian sermons, and extended explanations of liturgical actions are the essence of reverent worship. This attitude overlooks man's real need as a body-person for symbol, sign, and ritual action in expressing his religious sentiments.

The spoken word is not necessarily the best expression of a religious truth. Try to find an adequate verbal expression for a genuflection, a prayerful bow of the head, or the body position of kneeling. If found, do the words convey the fullness of meaning expressed by the action? We have to remind ourselves that the non-verbal communicates as eloquently, if not more so, than the spoken or written word.

The non-verbal, whether it is a well-orchestrated procession, a response period of meditative music, a colorful banner, expansive presidential gestures, a Gospel book covered in precious metal, the simplicity of an uncluttered sanctuary, flowing vestments, an aesthetically designed altar, the smell of incense, a pleasing ceramic or crystal chalice, bread that looks and tastes like bread, the positioning of candles, the presence of fresh flowers, etc., must be given ample opportunity to express beauty and reverence in its own particular way.

Worship as the act of the whole man should be a "multi-sensuous" action. We must be careful not to limit its expression just to the spoken and written word. The poetic richness of the non-verbal allows communication on a variety of levels. One action or sign conveys many meanings. We have to let these vital, non-verbal elements surface and flourish.

Christmas-Epiphany

The season of Christmas-Epiphany naturally lends itself to an abundance of visually orientated and dramatic involvement. Liturgically, we can let this season be for us a time of non-verbal renewal by improving our bodily gestures and liturgical signs. Para-liturgically, we can strive to incorporate better into our worship those traditions which are in harmony with the season. For example, a crib scene is quite compatible with the spirit of Christmas-Epiphany. It summarizes non-verbally the coming of Jesus into our world. In the past, the decoration of the crib has overpowered the liturgy. Zealous construction crews managed to cart in groves of trees, build larger than lifesize statues, and take over half the sanctuary. Such abuses cause one to wonder what the motif is saying theologically and liturgically. With regard to the liturgy, a hierarchy of values has to be respected.

Many churches have simple and devotional crib scenes that help people meditate on the mystery of the incarnation. A nativity scene appeals to people of all ages, from the young to the old. Children can pray to a God to whom they can easily relate. Parents can reflect on the mystery of God entering their lives through their own children. Grandparents can once again meditate that the Son of God became man to lead us to a fuller life.

Ideally the nativity scene would represent the theological reflection of the community. Perhaps each year a different committee could prepare the crib setting. This insures more variety in the design of the crib. The settings could be traditional, a contemporary motif, or styles illustrative of different cultures: Chinese, African, Mexican, Japanese, Dutch, Russian.

Some liturgy committees use the nativity scene as a visual transition between Advent and Christmas-Epiphany. The various readings for the Fourth Sunday of Advent, years A, B, and C, mention the quickly approaching birth of the Prince of Peace. It is on this Fourth Sunday of Advent that the liturgy committee has already set up the figures of Mary and Joseph standing near an empty manger. This scene, in its own non-verbal manner, quietly prepares the people for Christ's birth.

Christmas midnight Mass becomes the joyful occasion of the entrance of the Word of God into our lives. Many churches begin the midnight liturgy with a solemn proclamation of the Roman Martyrology for the 25th day of December. Should the community desire a more contemporary expression, a talented person from the parish could write a modern version for this year's Christmas.

A procession of parents and children carrying candles and accompanied with music and singing immediately follows the Martyrology. In front of the principal celebrant, a child carries the exposed book of the Word of God, another the Christ child. As the church lights slowly turn on, the procession passes the crib to place the Christ child to rest, and then continues into the sanctuary to celebrate the Liturgy of the Word.

The next occasion the community gathers is on the feast of the Holy Family. Once again, the nativity scene takes on new meaning reminding us of the importance of the family and its innate sacredness. On the feast of Epiphany, the star, wise men, shepherds and a few animals join the Holy Family. Over a four-week period, the nativity setting has told its story of the coming, birth, and adoration of the Child.

Banners

Another way the Christmas-Epiphany season can be enriched is through the use of banners. Some parishes make banners for the major seasons of the year, Lent, Easter, Pentecost, Advent, Christmas; others are in the habit of making a special thematic banner for each Sunday. This demands a great deal of dedication and artistic know-how, but the results are worth the time and energy. Banners can be incorporated into the liturgy in a number of festive ways: in processions, placed near the lectern or in the sanctuary, hung free, floating from the ceiling, or as a backdrop against a wall. However, there is one rule of thumb to follow in the creation of banners: make sure they are non-verbal representations. Non-verbal banners are harder to design but their effect is more intriguing and lasting. Excessively verbal banners like "He is born for us this day" are affronts to our imagination leaving little to challenge us or arouse our curiosity. One commodity the liturgy doesn't need is more words. For Christmas and Epiphany banner ideas, look in your local card shop. Magazines are also another valuable pictorial resources. It would be helpful if liturgy committees catalogued banner ideas for the season and feasts of the year so that a ready reference system could be available.

Christ as Gift; Our Response

The juxtaposition of the feasts of Christmas-Epiphany present many possibilities for the Christian community to witness their concern for their brothers and sisters in need. On Christmas, we celebrate the Father's gift of his Son to us. On Epiphany, we, like the shepherds and wise men who responded to God's gift of his Son, bow in awe presenting to Christ our personal gifts of person, community, and gold, frankincense, and myrrh. In imitation of their example, Epiphany is an opportune time to care for those in need of our personal assistance and support.

The *General Instruction,* section 101, is very explicit that such concern and witness be liturgically celebrated. It states:

> It is fitting that the participation of the faithful be expressed by their offering the bread and wine for the celebration of the eucharist, *together* with the other gifts for the need of the Church *and* of the poor.
> The offerings of the people are received by the priest, assisted by the ministers. The bread and wine for the eucharist are taken to the altar, and the other gifts are put in a suitable place.

The "together" . . . "and" parts of section 101 are still overlooked in too many parish liturgies. This is unfortunate because the *General Instruction* is attempting to revive a liturgical expression that is deeply rooted in the traditions of the early Church. As a Christian people we bear a responsibility to share of our abundance or of what we have with our brothers and sisters not so blessed.

Certain communities place large wicker baskets each Sunday in the church vestibule. These baskets are filled with clothing, non-perishable food, and other useful commodities. At the Preparation of the Gifts, these gifts for the poor or a particular charity are brought up with the other gifts. Later in the week, members of the parish take responsibility in distributing the gifts of the parish to those in need. Communities have found that this gesture helps to remind them that the mission of the Church is outward and service oriented. If such a recommended liturgical action is not presently practiced in your parish, then choose Epiphany, the celebration of our response to God's Gift, to begin such a non-verbal emphasis, and let it continue throughout the year.

Banners, crib scenes, candlelight processions, and gifts for the poor are some of the non-verbal ways of improving the Christmas-Epiphany season. Surely, you can come up with just as many. Be creative, plan out your ideas, and share them with others engaged in the important work of expressing the Word in Flesh.

The Uses of Slides in Liturgy

George Collopy

George Collopy is Art Director for Modern Liturgy *magazine.*

God spread His word through men. And those men used the communicating arts of their day to spread that word. They told stories, sang, danced, used music, art, anything to enhance the message. If Christ were to appear today isn't it conceivable that he would use the mass media? We are all TV oriented. Can't we borrow some of the huckster's thunder and spread the Good News through the same medium?

Let's talk about color slides, an easy, inexpensive way to get the message across. First of all try building a sense of community within your parish. In addition to praying for Mrs. Jones who suffered a heart attack recently, get a snapshot of Mrs. Jones and project it. Extend the thought with slides of wards in the local hospital or convalescent home. Make the prayer felt visually as well as orally. Announce banns of marriage with slides of the engaged couple; welcome the new baby to the community with his first photograph; introduce the new family in town with a slide of each member. The possibilities are endless.

Slides can also be programmed for creative liturgies and special occasions during the year. A baptismal ceremony could include color slides of the ocean, rivers, streams, reproductions of Biblical baptisms, etc. Don't overlook the marvelous possibilities found in various art books and periodicals. You can track the life of our Lord with all of the great masters of painting from Giotto through the Renaissance masters. Enhance the message of Christmas, the Passion, and Easter with color slides.

Consider slides for special liturgies. At St. Francis de Sales Cathedral in Oakland, California, special four week summer series on one theme are planned. One year, the subject was Play which centered on the necessity for all of us to "re-create." The homily on one of the four Sundays took the form of a slide presentation. A colorful handcut harlequin carried the message with blocks from a scrabble

117

game forming the sequences: "Time 2 see, Time 2 be = Time 4 play"; "Time 4 me, Time 4 God = Time 2 grow." The scrabble and harlequin sections were interspersed and illustrated with other thoughts; e.g. "Egg shells are sometimes so thin you may see out of one for a hundred years and never know you were inside"; "so BREAK OUT!" "Eggs-actly!" It is such play with words and visuals that homilies can be delivered with an effective punch.

Another year the theme was developed from the Simon and Garfunkel song "Everything's happening at the zoo, *I do believe.*" The slide presentation, which took the form of a non-verbal homily, explored the various cages into which people put themselves. This time, instead of art, color shots of real life scenes were used: people at the zoo looking into animal cages, tall iron gates, heavily barred windows, padlocked doors, telephone booths, No Trespassing signs, Keep off the grass, and the ultimate cage, a casket.

Parish financial reports have to be one of the dullest subjects foisted on the congregation all year. Usually the audience turns off after the subject has been announced. Since the subject is such a vital one we felt that the way to combat the apathy would be to adjust the message to another medium. For two successive years St. Francis de Sales has presented its financial report in the form of a silent slide show. The first "Bread on the Waters" presented all the pertinent facts, contributions, and disbursements with appropriate comparisons. Paper sculpture was used to illustrate some points. For other cases, actual location shots were taken to hammer away other considerations; i.e., a new roof for the rectory, new desks needed for the school. Loosely constructed, the show consisted of some 80 slides, all factual but treated in a very light vein. Appropriate music was also selected, "Pennies from Heaven." The true test of the presentation was shown in a 10% increase in revenue starting that Sunday and continuing throughout the year. This year we picked a definite theme for the financial report. Trading in on the popularity of "The Godfather" the title became "Panettone on the Waters." We spiced the figures and the problems with old photographs from the thirties, picked appropriate music from the same era and concluded with "Will you make us an offer we can't refuse." The response was very good.

Concerning the mechanics for producing slide shows, the easiest tool for the amateur is the Kodak Ektagraphic Visual Maker Kit. It retails for about one hundred dollars and consists of an instamatic camera and two copying stands. Art work, both flat and dimensional, can be prepared in two convenient sizes, 3 x 3 and 8 x 8.

In preparing your presentations, keep your plans within reasonable expectations. Above all, have a full-scale practice the night before. The liturgy is not the place to be working out cues and other bugs that will certainly need attention.

The Action of Breaking Bread

John P. Mossi, S.J.

The resurrected Christ is present in many signs: the assembled community, the Word of God, the eucharistic prayer, and one particular liturgical action that is receiving restored importance, the breaking of the bread. In the post-Easter passage of Luke 24, the two disciples of Emmaus were not able to "recognize" their fellow traveller until he took bread, gave the blessing, broke the bread and gave himself to them in a special way. Only at that point were the disciples' eyes opened and they "recognized him" (Luke 24:31). Upon meeting other disciples, "Then they told what had happened on the road, and how he was known to them in the breaking of the bread" (Luke 24:35).

The disciples knew that this pilgrim was the Lord because he unambiguously celebrated the actions of the Last Supper.

> *And he took bread, and when he had given thanks he broke it and gave it to them, saying, 'This is my body which is given for you. Do this in remembrance of me'* (Luke 22:19).

The disciples thought Jesus was dead; but in the breaking of the bread, they knew he was risen. In the spirit of the Emmaus disciples and following the command of Jesus, "Do this in remembrance of me," we also unite ourselves with Christ in his words and actions. We do what he did and celebrate his life. We take the bread, praise the Father for his constant love and everlasting mercy, we *break bread,* and distribute the bread as spiritual food for all to eat.

The Coverup

The task of restoring in our liturgy the significance of the breaking of the bread (also known as the fraction rite), is not an easy one because over the centuries it has been hampered by various historical events which have diminished its rich meaning and sign value. For example, in the early church, the community made the eucharistic bread which they presented to the celebrant at the presentation of the gifts. The use of real bread in the eucharistic celebration demanded that appropriate attention be given to the breaking of the bread. The celebrant was assisted by other priests and deacons at the fraction. In turn, acolytes helped distribute the broken bread to the assembly.

However, by the tenth century the breaking of the bread became relegated to a position of secondary importance. The fraction rite slipped quietly into insignificance with the introduction of unleavened bread—today, paper-thin hosts. Uniform, pre-broken, and mass-produced wafers became the accepted bread for use at the Lord's table. No longer did the faithful make the bread for use at the Lord's table. No longer did concelebrants or deacons assist at the fraction. The celebrant's pure white elevated host, instead of the one loaf of bread for the entire assembly, became the main liturgical focus. Gradually the bread was treated as an object to be looked at instead of what it actually was, food to be eaten. The host continued to receive excessive devotional attention. The faithful no longer received communion in the hand but only on the tongue. In time, the kneeling posture replaced traditional standing position as the ordinary manner to receive the Lord's bread. By the fourteenth century, the faithful seldom communicated. Attending Mass was reduced to seeing the host elevated. The essential meal actions of the liturgy became hidden and distorted.

Liturgical Update
In the majority of parishes, the major eucharistic actions of taking (presentation of gifts), blessing (eucharistic prayer), and giving (communion) of the Last Supper are sufficiently celebrated and understood. The breaking of the bread, still recovering from its token recognition in the old liturgy, is the last of the essential eucharistic actions to achieve its due prominence.

Not only is the fraction a liturgical action that is proper to the Lord's meal, it is also very rich in theological meaning. The breaking of the bread is a resurrectional sign of unity and reconciliation. For us, as it was for the disciples as Emmaus, it is a sign of Christ's presence. We associate ourselves with Christ by commemorating this memorial action of his. When the bread is broken, this event is an invitation for all to participate in the nourishment of the bread of life. Everyone by partaking of the one bread is intimately joined in Christ with one another. Likewise, the fraction reminds us that our divisions must cease so that Christ's spirit may visibly reign.

Saint Paul in I Corinthians 10:16-17 reflects on the meaning of the fraction for the early church.

> *The cup of blessing which we bless, is it not a participation in the blood of Christ? The bread which we break, is it not a participation in the body of Christ? Because there*

is one bread, we who are many are one body, for we all par-
take of the one bread.

For Paul the fraction signifies a new relationship between Christ
and the members of the assembly. The members of the assembly are
no longer individuals but the body of Christ. Christ, as the one bread,
is broken as the source of nourishment and unity for the church.

Guidelines

So far this article has treated the history and theology of the
fraction rite. The next stop is action. How can the parish or liturgy
committee proceed in revitalizing the rite of the breaking of the
bread? Fortunately, there are documents available that explicitly underscore the importance of the fraction rite in the liturgy.

The *General Instruction of the Roman Missal*, section 283,
which is located in the front section of the new sacramentary, states:

> *The nature of the sign demands that the material for*
> *the eucharistic celebration appear as actual food. The eu-*
> *charistic bread, even though unleavened and traditional in*
> *form, should therefore be made in such a way that the priest*
> *can break it and distribute the parts to at least some of the*
> *faithful. When the number of communicants is large or*
> *other pastoral needs require it, small hosts may be used.*
> *The gesture of the breaking of the bread, as the eucharist*
> *was called in apostolic times, will more clearly show the*
> *eucharist as a sign of unity and charity, since the one bread*
> *is being distributed among the members of one family.*

The *Third Instruction of the Correct Implementation of the Constitu-*
tion on the Sacred Liturgy sheds further light on the nature of the
bread and the fraction rite. Section five of the document states:

> *The truth of the sign demands that this bread look like*
> *real food which is broken and shared among brothers.*

> *The need for greater truth in the eucharistic sign is met*
> *more by the color, taste and texture of the bread than by its*
> *shape.*

> *Out of reverence for the Sacrament, great care and at-*
> *tention should be used in preparing the altar bread; it should*
> *be easy to break and should not be unpleasant for the faith-*
> *ful to eat. Bread which tastes uncooked, or which becomes*
> *dry and inedible too quickly, must never be used.*

> *Great reverence must also be used in breaking the con-*
> *secrated bread and in receiving the bread and wine, both at*
> *communion and in consuming what remains after commu-*
> *nion.*

These two documents are remarkable for their specific recommendations which provide the needed green light to go ahead and restore in a clear manner the breaking of the bread in liturgy. Besides referring to the importance of the fraction rite, both sources speak about the qualities of the eucharistic bread (notice that the word "bread" is employed, not hosts!). Bread is the normative food for use at Mass. It is described as "actual food," and "real bread." The bread is also to be made so that it can be broken. Why do the documents give such attention to the eucharistic bread? If the essential action of the fraction is to be restored in the liturgy, bread, and not hosts, has to be used so that the bread can in fact be broken. It is more imperative now than ever before that hosts be discontinued. A close look at section 283 of the *General Instruction* shows that hosts at present are restricted in their use. Hosts may be used: 1) when the number of communicants is large or 2) other pastoral needs require it. It should be carefully noted that even in these exceptional circumstances, the *General Instruction* says that small hosts "may be used." In other words, in the mind of these Roman documents, small hosts don't have to be used at all. At best, they are pastorally tolerated.

Immediately objections will be raised that to fully implement the spirit of these guidelines will only cause more problems on the parish level. For instance, who is going to make the bread? Won't the people, and perhaps the clergy, only be further confused? Isn't Mass long enough, do we have to add a fraction rite? And the litany goes on and on. These seemingly insurmountable obstacles should be balanced against some other important considerations. Why does the community gather to celebrate the eucharist? What meaning do the actions of the Last Supper have for the community? How clear are the liturgical signs? How historically faithful and liturgically correct is the celebration?

Hosts Out. Bread In

Here are a few practical steps that parishes can follow in improving the clarity of the fraction rite.

1. Through notices in the bulletin, various CCD and adult education classes, and a special homily on the theology of the eucharist, adequately instruct and prepare the community for the new level of celebrating the breaking of the bread.

2. If in the parish Masses real bread as recommended in the documents is not being used, then start a group of "papal bakers" to provide the eucharistic bread. Not only will this action be in concert with the spirit of the early church but it will bring increased meaning

to the local eucharistic celebration. The bread consecrated in the liturgy will truly be the community's bread.

3. Once the people are accustomed to the new bread, the fraction rite may be enhanced. When breaking the bread, the celebrant should hold the bread up for all to see. Break the bread slowly and reverently. It is very important that the assembly can clearly see that the bread is broken. Insure that the breaking action is in no way visibly hindered by ministers or altar items. If needed, other ministers should assist in the breaking of the bread.

4. In order to embellish the meaning of the breaking action, a short and appropriate passage from scripture can be read during the fraction. I Corinthians 10:16-17, John 6:35, Luke 24:30-31, 35 are some possible texts. Other fraction rite prayers and ideas can be found in the Paulist book, *Bread, Blessed and Broken,* edited by John Mossi, S.J. After a scriptural text or prayer, the congregation can then respond with a sung *Lamb of God* or an appropriate song with a bread theme.

5. If the chalice is to be extended to the assembly, the sign of unity can similarly be expressed with the wine by consecrating it in a single decanter. During the fraction rite, as the bread is being broken, wine from the one decanter is poured into chalices. In this way, the wine for the ministers and assembly comes from the same container. Should pouring wine from a decanter prove too difficult to execute, some wine from one chalice can be poured into the other chalices as an expression of unity.

Making Bread

Here are two recipes that make six round, flat loaves. Once you have mastered these recipes, adapt the formulas to the needs of larger celebrations.

A 1 ½ cup white flour
  ½ cup whole wheat flour
  1 ½ tsp. baking powder
  ½ tsp. baking soda
  ½ tsp. salt
  2 tsp. molasses
  1 cup buttermilk
  Combine ingredients, mix well. Knead with white flour. Shape into round form and place on greased cookie sheet. Bake at 350° for approximately 10-15 minutes. (Pre-heat oven.)
B 4 cups whole wheat flour
  1 ½ cups warm water

½ cup milk
2 tsp. salt
1 tbs. whole wheat germ
Dissolve salt, baking powder, and wheat germ in water. Add milk. Stir *into* the flour. (Save a little flour for later.) Remove dough from bowl and knead for ten minutes, adding liquid or flour as needed. Return dough to bowl, set aside for 4 hours. Butter cookie sheet and hands. Shape dough into six round, flat loaves. Bake in pre-heated oven, 375°, for 10-15 minutes. Let cool.

V
Musical Guidelines

The Four Hymn Mass?

John Melloh, S.M.

Rev. John Melloh teaches at Chaminade High School in Hollywood, Florida. Fr. Melloh has a Ph.D. in Historical Theology from St. Louis University.

The Church always needs reform. And Vatican II measured up to the task with a vigor that an ecclesiastical John F. Kennedy would have been expected to show. The cry for "full, conscious and active participation"—that primary consideration of the Council Fathers—started to get translated into pastoral and parochial projects of aggiornamento.

Eucharistic reform in the post-Vatican II Church has rejuvenated the structure of Christian Eucharistic celebration, from the call to worship through to the blessing of the People of God. Not only has the structure been modified, but the style of ritualization and of liturgical art has been changed. In fact, Vatican II gave birth to a new musical form of Eucharistic celebration—the four-hymn Mass.

In the ordinary parish in these United States, the four-hymn Mass has become almost normative. On Sunday after Sunday, the renewal in liturgical music has defined itself in the congregational singing of an Entrance Hymn, an Offertory Hymn, a Communion Hymn and a Concluding Hymn. We are now plagued with the four-hymn syndrome and quality liturgy is often measured against this new musical norm. I would like to comment on this phenomenon and offer some alternatives for parish celebrations.

The four-hymn Mass highlights four distinct parts of the celebration: the entrance and exit of the ministers, the offertory procession, and the communion of the people. The question I ask is whether these actions are the four primary parts of the celebration of the Eucharist. Are these truly deserving of solemnization by song? It is true that it is essential for the ministers to enter (and exit), but are these two processions of such a nature that they demand song, especially when the Eucharistic Prayer remains unclothed musically? Is the offertory procession as deserving of solemnity as the Memorial Acclamation of the people? Does the communion of the people demand singing as much as the responsorial psalm does?

In my experience with parish liturgical music, as well as with liturgical celebrations in religious communities, I have come to the conclusion that the four-hymn Mass is really not the most impressive contribution to the American Church in the era of liturgical revitalization.

Music in the liturgy serves two important functions. Music is an integral part of certain elements of the Eucharistic celebration; what I mean by that is that certain parts of the Eucharistic celebration are, by their very nature, songs; the texts themselves are lyrics, and so their rendering should be musical. They demand melody in order for their nature to be respected. For example, the responsorial psalm after the first reading is a song: the psalms are lyrical expressions of the Word of God. They demand melody for their expression. Did you ever wonder why the congregation has such a devil of a time trying to recite those interminably long antiphons and can't remember whether the text was "Lord" or "God" and stumbles through the responsorial Sunday after Sunday, distracting itself from prayer? If a good cantor were to sing the verses of the psalm, I'll bet the congregation could sing a simple refrain as the response, turning the responsorial psalm into a genuinely prayerful experience.

There is another important aspect which needs to be considered. Traditionally music has been used to accompany ritual actions. The old Introit Chant was the musical accompaniment for the entrance procession—the ritual of entering the church was accompanied by music. The Lamb of God was a litany-song which accompanied the lengthy and highly symbolic action of breaking the bread. At the Eucharistic celebration in times past, loaves of bread were used; the assistant ministers broke the bread immediately before distribution. A Sicilian Pope of Eastern descent, Sergius I, introduced the singing of the Lamb of God as a hymn to the victorious Lamb, slain yet standing, slaughtered yet life-giving. The song explained the action which was taking place. Didn't you ever feel that the Lamb of God— the way it is generally performed in the ordinary parish—recited by the congregation, tends to become a mere mouthing of words? Perhaps if melody were restored to it and a genuine fraction rite were reintroduced into the Eucharistic celebration, there could be "full, conscious and active participation." As it stands now, we have a song which is not sung, accompanying an action which is so minimal that it goes unnoticed.

Drawing on these two principles—that there are certain liturgical elements of the Eucharistic celebration which are musical by nature and that music serves an important function in accompanying ritual action—and holding to the fact that important elements in celebration should be highlighted within the structure of celebration, I should like to offer some practical suggestions for the reformation of the four-hymn Mass.

The Eucharistic Prayer is the center of the liturgical action of Eucharist. It is *the* great prayer of praise and thanksgiving. It is the heart, the center, the axis of Eucharistic action. How can we afford to allow the Great Prayer of praise to be recited (even worse, mumbled) —with no chance of being fittingly clothed musically? A Eucharistic Prayer, highlighted musically, assumes a position of importance, rightfully claimed. Within the present Roman ritual, there are three places in the Great Prayer which clamor for music: the Holy, the Memorial Acclamation and the Great Amen. These three acclamations are sung punctuations of the People of God, expressing their participation in the prayer which is being prayed in the name of the community gathered at the altar.

The Holy is the lyrical expression of the entire People of God of praise, thanksgiving, blessing, for the great deeds of Yahweh, performed for His people. These marvels have been retold in the Preface and the response of the Christian assembly is a full-bodied and full-throated singing of the hearty acclamation: Holy, holy, holy Lord, God of power and might. No Eucharistic celebration deserves that name if the Holy is not sung. The Holy is a song; its text is a lyric; it needs melody. Did you ever attend a birthday party and have "Happy Birthday" recited in unison by the assembled group? Probably not. But we Christian people of God will go on reciting the song "Holy, holy, holy Lord" till we're blue in the face and totally bored with the experience. And we'll wonder why. And we'll blame liturgy in general or liturgical reform in particular. And we'll be wrong if we do.

One of the fine reforms of the Eucharistic celebration in the Roman Rite has been the introduction of the Memorial Acclamation —the Anamnesis. Introducing "Christ has died. . . ." or one of the variants has given the congregation another chance to express communal faith and devotion, to participate vocally in the great Eucharistic Prayer being proclaimed by the presbyter, charged with offering blessing and praise to the Father in the name of the community. It is an acclamation; it is not a reading. It should burst forth exuberantly in a common song issuing from the lips and hearts of the gathered group, proclaiming—not reading, not reciting—the great mystery of faith. The Memorial Acclamation, when sung, highlights, clothes, and calls attention to the Great Thanksgiving Prayer.

One of the most important words in Christianity is "Amen." It is our special four-letter word! It is pregnant with meaning and can be a magnificent expression of shared faith. As the response to the Eucharistic Prayer, it is our affirmation of all that has been proclaimed to the Father by the presbyter acting in the name of the assembly; it is our saying "Yes, we believe" to all that is contained in the proclamation of the great deeds of Yahweh, from creation, to redemption, to the gift of the Spirit; it is our expressing a firm "So be it" to all that is demanded by our participating in the prayer—to the call to conversion, to filiation, to praise, to giving thanks. And so we shout "Amen."

Augustine, Bishop of Hippo, relates that there was so much faith evident in the great exclamation "Amen" shouted by his community at worship that that single word alone was responsible for many conversions to Christianity. And Justin the Martyr writes in his *Apology* that the acclamation "Amen" was like a clap of thunder. How emasculated, enfeebled and effete is our paltry response to the conclusion of the Eucharistic Prayer! Let the presiding minister sing "Through Him, with Him and in Him. . ." and let all the People of God thunder AMEN, giving voice to that shared faith, that communal joy, that demanding commitment which is expressed in celebrating.

This is where I think we should begin in reforming the four-hymn Mass: sing the Acclamations which highlight the Eucharistic Prayer. Start there—right at the very core of Christian celebration of the Eucharist. Surround the kernel of the mystery with joyful song.

After that is accomplished—a task which may take some time— then add more solemnity to celebrations by singing those other elements which need song: the responsorial psalm and the alleluia— which, again, are songs; and who can merely recite "Alleluia?"—the Lamb of God—a litany-song, which can be sung by the choir, with the congregation singing the refrain; the Lord's Prayer—that prayer of forgiveness and reconciliation, fully eschatological, proclaiming our destiny as a Christian community, and the concluding acclamation to the "Deliver us. . . ."

Then ice the cake with the sung entrance song and recessional. Then on to the accompaniment of the offertory procession with song; forward to the communion hymn—but only after the essentials have been taken care of.

Some Thoughts on Writing Songs

Dr. Laverne Wagner

Laverne Wagner is chairman of the music department at Quincy College in Quincy, Illinois. He is also music editor of the Pray Together monthly missal.

These reflections are presented with the hope that they will be helpful to those persons who are interested in writing new songs for the liturgy today. When Vatican II sanctioned a vernacular liturgy, I am sure no one foresaw in all its dimensions the demand which would be created for new music. Liturgical musicians today have been composing music to fill this need. Like all music written for specific needs, some of this is better than the remainder. While we cannot guarantee a masterpiece from every song-writing attempt, we do want to offer some hints which can be of help in getting that melody going around in your head sung and loved by other Christians.

A song can begin to take shape from any one of its components: text, melody, harmony, or rhythm. If you do start with a melody, eventually there will have to be some appropriate words with it, and perhaps some of these might occur to you while humming over the melody, or the rhythm might suggest them.

The text is frequently a point from which to start a song. A favorite place for finding appropriate thoughts which can be molded into verse is still the Bible. From the time of King David the Psalms have been a rich source of inspiration. However, the Psalms we read in English are translations, and very seldom is it possible to take this translation and set it word for word. The more usual manner is to paraphrase the Psalm texts. This usually means setting them into English verse with its regularly recurring accented and unaccented syllables. It is a good idea to get a workable rough draft of the text first. Undoubtedly, there will have to be some changes made as the song develops, but there has to be a starting place, and when dealing with such an abstract art as music one has to have something as concrete as possible from which to proceed.

133

Now we need a melody. This is undoubtedly the most important thing in the song. Some people seem to have a natural gift for writing beautiful melodies. Every melody is a highly personal expression. From where do they come? I always remember that medieval picture of the Holy Spirit in the shape of a dove whispering Gregorian chant melodies into the ear of St. Gregory the Great, Pope from 590-604. Mozart used to thoughtfully improvise at the clavier (piano or harpsichord), while mentally composing his works. Beethoven kept a sketchbook in which he notated his melodies while he walked around the Vienese countryside. We know that sometimes even these famous composers got desperate. Haydn used to pray for inspiration. Mozart threw dice, each number standing for a different pitch. Today we know of some pieces that have been composed by taking telephone numbers and transforming each number into the corresponding pitch of the scale, number one translating as do, or C, number two as re, or D, etc. These facts are pointed out to remind you that inspiration may, but does not always have to be, the basis for writing an interesting melody. I have found that melodies are very fleeting things, and when an interesting one occurs it must be captured right then and there, or it will disappear into the realm from which it came. Certain situations, or even times of the day, seem to be conducive to bringing good melodies. Like other creative thoughts, melodies may come easier upon first waking from a restful sleep. To capture these fleeting melodies a cassette recorder in a handy, convenient place is very helpful. Of course, it is always possible to come up with some kind of an original melody if circumstances require it, no matter what the time, place, or situation may be. But we are thinking especially of catchy, interesting ones.

In speaking of the tape recorder, we should mention that you could, in fact, compose your whole song directly on a cassette tape. However, eventually it will have to get translated into musical notation if very many persons other than yourself are ever to sing it. It is only after a song gets put into musical notation that it can easily be revised, changed, and re-written. You can expect that some of this will be necessary. Very seldom, and for very few people, do the words and melody arise spontaneously, fully and completely developed, needing no revision. I have had some experience with persons who claim to have this kind of inspiration. Usually what they consider to be a fully developed song could have been much improved with revisions. Either that, or it is a rather dull and uninteresting product which is better forgotten.

This brings up another point. If you are interested in writing songs, and if you are really serious about making your contribution to Christ's praise and worship in this manner, you should expect to develop this ability over a considerable period of time. It is a common mistake to expect every one of your songs to be a masterpiece, which is going to revitalize Christianity and bring you fame and fortune in the process. All the good song writers whom I know, or of whom I have ever heard or read, have made hundreds of attempts, and had a few successes. Note that when a well-known song writer dies you find mentioned the few melodies for which he is famous. A whole lifetime of work is summed up in these few enduring melodies.

Songs in our culture have harmony as well as melody. The ability to use chords correctly is a skill which has to be learned. It consists of much more than being able to name the correct pitches for any chord. The real art is in the manner in which one chord follows another. Eventually every successful song writer has to learn his art, because the harmonization of the song frequently contributes much to its general effect. The harmony cannot just be left to chance, or to be filled in by someone else.

Some further observations should be made about the make-up of songs. Once they are placed in musical notation it is readily apparent if they fit into patterns of symmetry and balance which are aesthetically satisfying. Songs which come out in irregular numbers of measures such as seven, nine, thirteen, fifteen, and so on, are usually not so satisfying. Phrases of two, four, and eight measures are the norm, and choruses of 16, 24, and 32 measures are still common. Irregular songs usually sound as though some note is not held long enough, or something should be repeated which is not, or something which is extra should be deleted. This is not to condemn irregular songs . . . rather to suggest that this is not the place for an inexperienced writer to start.

The text usually fits to the melody in a relationship of one syllable of text to one note of music. Sometimes a few notes of music may be slurred, having only one syllable, but this should be the exception rather than the rule, unless one is striving for some special effect. Problems frequently arise when setting several verses to the same music. It should almost never be necessary to add notes, or to take out notes of the melody in order to get the text to fit for the various verses. If you doubt this statement, just examine carefully the works in a good hymnal such as the Episcopal Hymnal 1940, a classic compilation of sacred music. Another point to note carefully is the relationship between stressed and unstressed syllables of the text and the melody. Words such as "the," "and," and unstressed syllables of longer words, do not belong on the strong counts of a measure, or the stressed pitches of a melody. They could lead to a real distortion of meaning of the text, besides making for uncomfortable singing. Words and music must flow and mold naturally together.

Now after having composed your song, what to do with it? The first impulse is to send the musical notation as a single line melody, with words underneath the notes and guitar chord symbols above, to a publisher. It would be much better to send a version with organ accompaniment (which will eventually have to be made anyway), and also to send along a cassette tape of a performance of the song. It is well to note that professional song writers always make a demonstration recording of songs they are serious about selling. The manner of performing a song may even be very crucial to its effect, and a performance should help correct any ambiguity which might still remain after a consideration of the musical notation.

I am sure that most persons who write that first song and submit it to a publisher have high hopes for their artistic endeavor. Then when they receive a rejection they are crestfallen. It is quite an expensive matter to get a song out in published form. Publishers have to invest their resources carefully. They may like your song and still not accept it due to space, timeliness, or any one of other innumerable legitimate reasons.

The American Society of Composers, Authors, and Publishers, commonly called ASCAP, has done a good job of implanting in composers' minds the thought that they should receive royalties from musical works they may have published. Certainly this is true for composers of established reputations in the popular as well as the serious music fields. However, for someone who has just written his first religious song to place himself on this same level is, at least in my mind, a little presumptuous. Rather than expecting a royalty check, it would probably be more practical to consider selling your song outright for a flat fee. Fifty to one hundred dollars are some common fees for excellent usable songs which show some promise. While you may not agree with, or like, this suggestion, I would remind you that royalties are based on sales, and you cannot expect to sell many printed copies of a religious song. It is a fact of today's musical practice that most Catholic churches would rather mimeograph the words, sometimes also the music, of your song and distribute it to their congregations this way than buy printed copies. The fact that this is illegal and morally unjust is apparently not going to stop it from being done. I can only see this practice as the reflection of a tight-fisted, dollar-and-cents attitude which would like to hold that music is an unnecessary frill in worship. This same attitude existed before Vatican II. There was never any money for music in the church budget then, either. The result is situations like that of James Theim, the composer of the well-known song, *Sons of God,* who received exactly $40.17 in royalties during 1967, a year when the song was at the height of its popularity.

Good luck to you, and I hope you create many masterpieces in your songs. Our church has use for all of them.

Music as Prayer

Eileen Freeman

Eileen Freeman is a Ph.D. candidate in scripture at Notre Dame. She is also interested in church music and is an accomplished guitarist.

Have you ever wondered exactly what there is about music that makes it as universal a phenomenon as language itself? Every society on earth, whether complex or extremely simple, has some form of music indigenous to it. Even the most "primitive" groups have serious, often ancient musical traditions. Incredible varieties of instruments accompany the countless songs which the world sings—gourds, bones, reeds, teeth. No matter what form it takes, music seems to be a cultural constant of humanity.

This is not a new phenomenon; man has been a music-maker ever since he has been leaving records of himself. Religious music, love songs, funeral dirges, work songs and national anthems all survive from as long ago as 4000 B.C. in Sumeria and Egypt. As much as twenty percent of the Bible is really song: not only the Psalms, but also the Canticle of Canticles, the songs of Deborah (Judges) and Moses (Exodus), and many parts of the prophets were designed to be sung. In fact, many of the Psalms even have musical directions for their performance. Centuries before the birth of Jesus, the Greek philosophers had taken note of mankind's musical heritage, and had tried to devise a scientific explanation for it. After complex experiments with vibrations and sounds, they concluded that the source for music is in mankind's "soul," not in his "thought."

When we look over the world's musical past, we can see that from the beginning, one of the primary uses of music was in worship. The earliest hymns are devoted to many different gods and goddesses; they express reverence, fear, trust, gratitude, a whole catalog of human emotions. The Jews sang their psalms and sacred songs to Yahweh. Their descendents, the early Christians, sang those psalms, too, adding their own hymns to Christ the Savior. It is widely believed that the beginnings of Colossians I and Philippians 4 are prose settings of Christian hymns, as are the canticles of Zachary, Mary and Simeon. There is even a whole church "hymnal" from the second century, sometimes called the Odes of Solomon, which is full of exquisite lyrics. In one song, "directions" are given to the vocalists:

> Let the singers sing the grace of the Lord most High,
>   And let them bring their songs before Him;
> Let their gentle voices be like the majestic beauty of the
> Lord And let their heart be like the Day

Saint Paul not only urged the churches he pastored to sing the praise of God, he expected the Spirit to inspire some people with gifts of improvising musical prayers (see 1 Cor. 14).

Unfortunately, as the world was plunged into the darkness of barbarian invasions and the Middle Ages, this intimate relationship between music and prayer began to be obscured. Monastic and canonical choirs sang in the name of the people, so that during the liturgy in many places, the people were not invited to pray via music. We still feel the effects of all this somewhat in America. A great many parishes have grown up with no musical tradition at all or with a poor one. Surprising numbers of people have had literally no experience combining music and praise. Happily, that situation is being remedied.

Why should music and prayer always have been such inseparable companions? Music, that is, rhythm and melody, involve the cooperation of our voices, our bodies, our intellect and the whole range of our human feelings. In other words, the best music inevitably sums up what we are; it unites all our human faculties. Think for a moment of some song that is a prayer for you. Sing it carefully. Now. Stop reading this article, and pray that song. . . . You see how intent your mind was on the lyrics, trying to extract every ounce of meaning from them. Your heart, your feelings and emotions deepened; if the song was especially powerful, you felt it even in your fingertips. Your body either tensed up, paying close attention to the prayer, or it relaxed and went limp. Ultimately, your faith bound together all these parts of you by giving its assent to the prayer. In short, your sung prayer has succeeded in gathering together all that makes you human.

We want to "get it together" when we pray; we want to be attentive. We are well aware that Jesus is God, and that our comprehension of him is quite limited. When God speaks to us in prayer, he does not do so (normally) in an audible manner; we have to listen carefully or we shall be deaf to his word. By singing our worship of God, we join all our powers together to hear and to seek him.

I think, too, that music is a powerful and a culturally acceptable way of expressing our deepest feelings. I have noticed at Mass that many people who would never "participate" in things like offertory processions and lector programs will be vocally demonstrative when it comes to singing. I have also met people whose understanding of the Mass is limited or just starting to grow, for whom the music at Mass is their only way of praying from the heart. A song can take a difficult scripture text and not only re-present it to a congregation, but can make the reading a real prayer experience or predispose people to pray. Prayer that is sung has a way of keeping people awake and alert, and of making spoken responses much more alive.

Liturgical Ramifications

Since musical prayer can make (or break) a celebration of the Eucharist, the role of the minister of music in choosing suitable pieces is a crucial one. I would like to speak about sung prayer in the liturgy in the practical context of the music minister's function.

Consider, for a minute, a liturgy in honor of St. Francis-Who-Loved-the-Birds. The opening prayer is the celebrant's own adaptation of Shelley's *Ode to a Nightingale*. The readings are taken from Audubon's bird book and from the Gospel text of Jesus' baptism (where the Holy Spirit appears like a dove!). What a ludicrous (or blasphemous) idea, you say. True—but is it any more ridiculous than the musician who chooses *I am a Rock* and the *Sounds of Silence* for Mass music because he wants people to be "relevant" and to think about lost, despairing humanity? To use music which focuses all our energies on sin and despair and not on the loving Lord who heals despair and forgives sin, is not prayer—it is the very antithesis of prayer. Such music is not even likely to dispose a congregation for prayer.

All of this leads up to the basic axiom: The essential quality of any music done at a liturgy is that it be prayer-full music. This means that it should draw people's attention clearly and ultimately to God in some way that is suitable for a given liturgy and the needs of the people. This does not mean it must be addressed to God directly; *A Mighty Fortress* is in the third person, yet the power of the words and music has led many to experience a deeper faith in the power of God. Just the opposite thing happens in the third verse of an otherwise good song called *I Lift up my Eyes*. The verse says, "Oh God, if you love your people, don't leave them alone." What it clearly implies is that it is possible for God not to love his people; that he is capable of abandoning them if he chooses. What a horrible prayer to offer to someone whose faith needs strengthening!

A musical prayer that is successful has clearly understood lyrics along with a melody that has the potential of involving a person's whole being. Abstruse symbolism is a nuisance; if people can't instantly understand a symbol, they will stop singing (and praying) and watch the musicians perform instead. Could you join in a prayer that began "Supreme confluence and efficient cause of the cosmos, in which the ontology of our being. . . ."? For that matter, can you *instantly* comprehend and *pray* the following lyrics: "Go ahead and hate your neighbor," from *One Tin Soldier,* or "I'll be a dandy and I'll be a rover," from *Today?* Even if the lyrics are prayerful, good music is important, too, in setting the mood for the prayer. How involved would your prayer be if every hymn were set to the tune of *The Bear Went Over the Mountain?*

A rule of thumb for all who have the responsibility of choosing the music which a congregation will be praying at a liturgy: Only offer a song for worship after you yourself have personally lived with that song, prayed it, dissected it and made it flesh of your flesh, and let God speak his word to you through it.

A second rule of thumb: All music ministers should pray that they grow in faith. If a song proves good both musically and prayerfully, but you cannot in faith sing it, you should consider getting some help in choosing music, perhaps from the celebrant, if feasible, lest the congregation be given inadvertently music unsuitable for them. There is no crime in asking for help on this matter—we are the Body of Christ and ought to care for each other's needs.

The minister of music (and all parish music ministries) will be completely, totally and unequivocally ineffectual in choosing prayerful music suitable for a liturgy unless he or she spends time daily in personal prayer. The reason for this is obvious: a dry well cannot give water to anyone. I find it helpful to sing spontaneously when I pray; to "let the Spirit" help me pray. Singing spontaneously not only opens me up to more and better musical talents, it also makes me more sensitive to the whole notion of music as prayer.

When the minister of music is sensitive to the Lord's voice, he or she will be drawn instinctively to prayerful music, and will grow in the knowledge of what is pastorally most suitable for the group he serves. For example, the Carpenters sing a song called *I Won't Last a Day Without You.* The refrain says, "When there's no getting over that rainbow, when my smallest of dreams won't come true, I can take all the madness the world has to give, but I won't last a day without you." I love this song; I often use it for my personal prayer. I can sing it to the Lord; he is the one without whom I cannot last a day. But although the song moves *me* deeply, I know that pastorally this piece of music is not what my parish needs; it is too symbolic, too feminine, and musically, too difficult. On the other hand, *Day by Day* and *Just a Closer Walk* express much the same prayer and are more accessible to my parish.

A third rule of thumb: All those responsible for the music a congregation sings or listens to are the servants of that congregation and ought to be only interested in what the congregation needs. Notice that I said NEEDS, not WANTS. A congregation might want *On This Day O Beautiful Mother* for Good Friday, but that is obviously not what they need on that particular occasion.

A Scenario:

A church musician arrives at the borders of heaven, guitar (or baton or Buxtehude's *Praeludium and Fugue)* in hand, only to find that his passport is not complete. He goes back to earth to fix things up. "What did I do?" he wails to his congregation. They respond, "I needed to pour out my heart in praise of God—and you had the choir sing a sacred anthem in my name." "I needed to tell God I loved him, and you told me sarcastically to go ahead and hate my neighbor." "I needed to repent and you told me to be a dandy and a rover."

If a song is prayer-filled and is pastorally good, it also ought to be musically good, not trite, and within the range of the congregation. If a song is unsingable, it is also unprayable. No person in the pew who is faced with an unusually high or technical piece will be able to sing and pray at the same time. What is within the range of sisters in a convent will not always be within the range of thirty men on a cursillo. Fourth graders can sing much more easily than pre-adolescents whose voices are changing. For these reasons new music must be rehearsed before Mass, maybe even for a couple of weeks. You cannot throw a congregation into the water without a life preserver (i.e., a rehearsal) and expect them to flounder and pray at the same time. However, if a hymn or other kind of music (like a Holy or an Amen) is prayerful, pastorally suitable and musically good, then all those who are at the liturgy where it is sung will be able to pray and to worship God together.

When prayer and music unite, the result is glorious. I have never known a congregation to want to sing trite, unprayerful music once they had been exposed to what musical prayer can be. Blaise Pascal once wrote that there is a "God-shaped vacuum" in the heart of every human being. The musician who can tap into that vacuum, ministering God's grace and healing to a congregation through music, is performing an invaluable service for the Body of Christ. May the Lord raise up composers, lyricists, singers, and musicians deeply rooted in faith and love to lift his people to him with a glad cry, "Hallelujah! Praise the name of the Lord!"

A Musical Prayer

> Teach me the songs of your truth, oh Lord,
>> That I may produce fruits in You;
> And open to me the music of your Holy Spirit
>> That, with every note I may praise you
> Out of your abundant kindness, grant me this
>> For you are sufficient for all our needs
>>> Hallelujah!

(from the Odes of Solomon, ca. A.D. 150)

Practicality in Folk Formation

Larry Brown

*Rev. Larry Brown is diocesan director of folk music in the
diocese of Wheeling. He is also director of the "S.P. Foundation," a group which travels throughout the diocese giving
concerts and workshops.*

Many particulars are always "taken for granted" in any situation, whether it be life, relationships, music, and for us—forming a
parish folk group. So often, we are "turned-off" or "tuned-out" at
the liturgy by musicians, who in all honesty, are trying their best to
help us sing praise to God. What is the problem that surrounds this
situation?

In my experience as a parish priest involved in folk music, and
having organized three parish folk groups, the problem is one of *practicality*.

The aspect of gathering together the available musicians in the
parish and fitting them into a group is done with little or no foresight
on the part of the priest or leader-moderator. Some helpful hints are
very necessary. The basic objective is to have a group that can *work*
together, blend-in instruments, voices, and rhythm-strumming (this
comes naturally after a period of time working together!!).

The object is to teach the musicians all the aspects of presentation, so that they will know how to lead the congregation. This is accomplished by many weeks of preparation and practice before the notion of playing for a liturgy. Each member must become familiar with
the other as to the style, strum, and music background of each
member of the group. In this way, all come to develop an ease which
comes from knowing each one's method. Eventually this develops
into what I call a "group style" of playing.

Two or three hours a week is a good amount of time that should
be given by all for rehearsing, and this goes on as long as the group is
together. There has never been a substitute for rehearsals. When the
group is solidified, it is now time to begin assigning roles within the
group. After weeks of practice, individuals tend to express a variety
of qualifications for necessary roles. I firmly believe that each

144

member, whether a musician or vocalist, should have duties and responsibilities.

For example, the following is done before the liturgy: one musician, usually the lead guitarist, takes care of tuning all the guitars and instruments; another takes care of the library of music and setting up the music for the liturgy; another handles the PA System and checks the volume, microphones, and all electronic equipment. These "trivia" are often "taken for granted" by many groups. A little check list before the liturgy is a sure reward!

But the backbone of any folk group is the INPUT of the leader-moderator, who must accomplish all of the above. His leadership and direction leads the group to understand the role that they play in the liturgy both spiritually and musically. It should be evident that a group cannot function from week to week without his thrust. In many cases, that is the reason why so many folk masses "die-out" in parishes—lack of direction! The moderator should work with the group to choose the songs in theme with the liturgy and to see that they can be learned both by themselves and the congregation. In some circumstances, the group does not know the schedule of music until 15 minutes before the beginning of the liturgy—thus utter chaos results—the congregation knows after one measure that the group is uncertain and does not know the music!

The moderator-leader of the parish folk group should have knowledge of the liturgy, liturgical folk music, and sources upon which to draw. In other words, he should know more than the group, if he expects to lead them to a beautiful liturgy.

Another factor in practicality of forming a parish folk group is to begin by learning folk music that is relatively simple, both for the group and the congregation. A building-up process is required for both. Beginning with less difficult music rules out frustration on the part of the group, who may never have seen this music before. Remember, liturgical folk musicians are not born!

Therefore, it is a good policy to use all available resources in the media to reach this process. In the parishes that I have served, I bought all the folk music and records to show the group how the song is played and written. This does away with guessing. Another helpful hint is to catalog your music according to liturgical season and place within the liturgy, such as entrance hymn, acclamations, communion and recessional hymns.

These are a few of the basics in the practicality of forming a parish folk group that I have learned to use in my experience as a musician and leader. I am happy to say that they have never failed me yet! If someone were to approach me and ask how to form a group, my answer, in short would be for them to:

1. Find a dedicated leader-moderator—essence of unity.
2. Find musicians who are willing to give selflessly.
3. Practice, practice, practice.
4. Have enthusiasm and initiative.
5. Have defined roles and direction for each member.

As a result, I think we could avoid the last minute disasters and phone calls on the night before the liturgy, and most of all, a group of musicians meeting for the first time in the sanctuary.

Permission Versus Xerox Machine

Carol Fay

*Carol Fay teaches high school religion and directs the folk
group at St. Joseph's Parish, East Rutherford, New Jersey.*

In this age of stress on congregational participation in the liturgy, priests, cantors, choir directors, and church musicians are fran-
tically searching for music that our congregations can sing easily. As
quickly as our modern composers are able to write good music, it is
picked up by these hungry consumers and mimeographed in parish
houses across the country. The composers and publishers are being
xeroxed out of their rightful pay.

In the United States artists are not subsidized by the government, so they are forced to write, paint, sing, etc. for a *buying* public.
Each time a composer's piece is performed for profit, or the text or
music is duplicated (whether for profit or not), the performer or
group using the music must obtain permission to use the artist's
work. The legal rights to this art have been secured under the international copyright law, the federal copyright law, or both.

Copyright law was developed before the invention of the Xerox
machine, but there have always been processes available for repro-
ducing printed words and music. Even if copied by hand, it is against
the law to reproduce copyrighted material without permission from
the owner of the copyright. Composers and publishers will normally
grant permission provided some important conditions are fulfilled.
Some form of payment for use of the music is usually required, for
obvious reasons. Even more important than payment though, the
copyright must be protected. This means that copies made must carry
the copyright notice, date, and owner in exactly the same form as it
appears on the original composition. If someone innocently removes
the copyright notice on a piece of music, makes hundreds of copies
without the notice, and distributes the copies, the composer's legal
rights to his own composition become jeopardized. What a cruel blow
against someone who went to the trouble and expense to share a rare
talent with others. Yet if you look in a few random parish hymnals,

147

you will have difficulty locating the copyright holder of most of the music.

We consumers of church music seem to have given ourselves a generous exemption from copyright law. We freely duplicate and distribute copies of the music of Wise, Parker, Repp, Miffleton, and a host of others for use in our parishes. We proclaim "It is all for non-profit use!"—as we reach into the pocketbooks of our contemporary composers.

On the other hand, how can a parish pay every time it copies a song? The need for flexibility in parish use has been met by several companies by means of annual reprint licenses. For a set fee a parish may print any music published by the contracted company for a period of one year. F.E.L., N.A.L.R., Resource Publications, and others offer this particular arrangement. Several other publishers have different plans available so that each parish may have the use of a wide variety of music printed within the law, and making sure that the composer and publisher get paid.

The most time consuming part of putting together a "legal" parish hymnal is finding the addresses of the companies whose music you are using. For some of the addresses it may be necessary to go to a public library reference desk and look up the publisher's name in the *Index of Music Publishers*. Most of the addresses you will need are listed below:

Alba House, Canfield OH 44406
Barnegat Music, 720 7th Ave., New York NY 10036
Beechwood Music, 1750 Vine, Hollywood CA 90028
F.E.L., 1925 Pontius Ave., Los Angeles CA 90025
G.I.A., 7404 S. Mason Ave., Chicago IL 60638
Irving Music, 1416 N. LaBrea, Hollywood CA 90028
Jan-Lee Music, 260 El Camino Dr., Beverly Hills CA 90212
Lexicon Music, Box 296, Woodland Hills CA 91364
NY Times Music, 10 E. 53rd St., New York NY 10022
N.A.L.R., 2110 W. Peoria Ave., Phoenix, AZ 85029
Raven Music, 4107 Woodland Pk N, Seattle WA 98103
Resource Publications, P.O. Box 444, Saratoga CA 95070
St. Francis Prod., 1229 S. Santee, Los Angeles CA 90015
Vanguard Music, 250 W. 57th St., New York NY 10019
Weston Priory Prods, Weston VT 05161
World Library, 2145 Central Parkway, Cincinnati OH 45214

The letter to the publisher should be something like the following:

Dear Publisher:

We are planning a parish music program and would like permission to include the following songs to which you hold the copyright in our hymnal.

> Title — Composer
>
> Title — Composer
>
> Title — Composer

We intend to duplicate the words only, and will require about 700 copies. The songs will be used to enhance congregational singing in our church. Please grant permission or send information explaining the steps necessary to obtain permission.

Sincerely yours, etc.

There is no general formula for the cost of reprint permission. Each company has its own program. Our parish recently completed a hymnal containing 180 songs for an original outlay of about $250.00 for permissions. That works out to less than 36¢ per copy. More expense is involved for paper and ink, etc., and still more if the hymnal is to have a plastic cover, or if an expensive printing job is done, but that is not necessary. What is necessary is that the people have the words so that they can sing, and that these words have been provided for them legally and honestly. If we are to expect continued good music for good liturgies, we must be willing to pay for it.

VI
Drama in the Sanctuary

Liturgical Drama

Michael E. Moynahan, S.J.

Fr. Moynahan is presently pursuing a graduate degree in Drama and Theology at the Graduate Theological Union.

I. What is it?

If I were to draw a picture depicting a typical Roman Catholic liturgy, it would consist of a gigantic mouth overwhelming a tiny ear. Talk! Talk! Talk! So much of our liturgy is simply verbal, and poor verbiage at that! As celebrators of God's covenant we have lost contact with our visual and ritual roots. Liturgical drama is an attempt to rediscover them.

Liturgical drama tries to engage the whole person, not just our ears. It attempts to allow us to respond totally to the Good News. This means not just in a logical or reasonable way, but as a thinking/feeling person. Liturgical drama tries, with all the means available, to let the Word become flesh in the seventies. Through the use of drama, in the context of the liturgy, we attempt to communicate the Word of God as clearly and as powerfully as possible.

Jesus used stories (parables) in his day to spark the imaginations of his audience and capture their hearts. His images were clear, familiar and effective. He used the best means available to communicate his message. Jesus touched people. He comforted them. He spoke to them. He listened to them. He laughed, got angry and enjoyed a party as much as the next fellow.

Dramatization is one of the means we have been given whereby we can capture some of the warmth, the feeling and the spirit of the man Jesus. Just as Jesus' stories could captivate his audiences and communicate his message, so too dramatizations are powerful modern means for us to reclaim congregations and allow the Good News to be proclaimed in new and powerful ways.

Actions Speak Louder than Words

At the last supper, before Jesus began his teaching on love and service, St. John tells us that he got up from the table and washed the feet of his friends. After this ritual of service, and only after it, did Jesus talk to his friends about the significance of his actions. After washing he talked about why he washed.

Actions so often say more than mere words. And they don't always have to substitute. It doesn't have to be an "either/or" situation with words and dramatic action. They can support one another and in this way allow the Word to be proclaimed more effectively.

We can talk about love and we can actually love. It's the difference between homilizing and dramatizing. "Talk is cheap. Whisky costs money!" "Put your money where your mouth is!" "Put up or shut up!" These slogans point to the possible disparity between what we say and what we do. Jesus' death on the cross was the most eloquent and moving statement he could make about love for someone else. It paled in one sense, and yet reinforced and substantiated everything he had ever said about love.

Week after week we hear another installment from one of the four gospel writers. Out of habit we nod our heads as Jesus continues to do his good deeds. Overworked medium and poor transmission combine each week to uncover new ways of rendering the Good News impotent. Jesus not only spoke about caring for others, he showed us how to care by giving sight to the blind, by restoring hearing to the deaf, speech to the dumb, strength of legs to the lame and feeling to the stone-hearted. How much of this is conveyed or affects us through the Sunday rendering of the gospel?

Engagement

There is a California Jesuit who travels around the country with his little circus. His name is Fr. Nick Weber. His work is creator, director and ringmaster for the smallest circus in the world: The Royal Lichtenstein Quarter Ring Side Walk Circus. I had the opportunity of working three months with him. During that time I experienced how you can touch people, heal people through drama and the circus.

In the circus we engaged not just the congregation's ears, but their eyes, their smell, their feelings, in a word—the heart. And in this way we somehow freed their spirit to respond and celebrate. We taught them by showing them how wonderful surprise is: Christmas trees from crumpled newspaper, doves from popped balloons and ducks from oven roasted birds.

The spoken word in the circus was appropriately wedded to action. The result was learning, laughing, shedding a tear of melancholy or joy, celebrating life, and somehow leaving the circus feeling richer and wiser than when you came. Can the same be said by those who attend our Sunday liturgies? Are they really celebrations? How many of our worshippers do we engage in liturgy? Just the head or the whole person?

We have to engage more than the ears and minds of our worshippers. The more senses engaged in liturgy, the more powerful and complete the liturgical experience can be. And this is no magic formula. It is just good sense.

Drama utilizes many senses and appeals to the complete person. Consider the ways Jesus healed people—word and action, speaking and touching. Words can be misleading, even equivocal at times. Actions, gestures, a worked-out mime, are all powerful proclamations in their clarity, brevity and simplicity.

II. Types of Liturgical Drama

There are at least seven types of liturgical drama. Some forms run dangerously close, if not over, into another's area. There can be multiple variations in specific kinds of liturgical drama. We will examine some of these possibilities as we look at each drama type. The seven forms of drama are: interpretive proclamation, group interpretive proclamation, mime, improvisation, psycho-drama, scene or story dramatizations, and the total dramatic liturgical experience. Let's take a look now at each form and its potential liturgical use.

1. *Interpretive proclamation* consists of one person vocally presenting, interpreting and proclaiming the scriptural "good news" to us. It is more than a dull recitation of meaningless words and phrases. It is not mumbling or bungling your way through an unfamiliar passage from the Bible. It is using all the gifts God has given you in the range, depth, pitch and resonance of your voice and helping the Word come to life.

Too often, timid lectors feel any type of reading that departs from deadening monotone is totally out of place. Many potentially good lectors are unfairly intimidated by those who might fault his energetic proclamation as "over-doing it," "hamming it up," "acting," "entertaining us instead of helping us to pray." We have to remember that when our congregation has been hypnotized, lulled into an etherizing sleep by the monotonous murmurings of the unskilled at the lectern, they will be shocked and disturbed by any scripture that falls upon their ears above a whisper. Perhaps if we had some men and women lectors who would use their voices fully to proclaim God's Word to us, we'd put down those distracting and menacing missalettes once and for all.

Interpretive proclamation is evocative. It demands a response. Through it, a skilled lector can vocally command the attention of the congregation and dispose them to listening and responding to the Word of God. He can try to capture the different characters with his voice; e.g., the calmness and straightforwardness of the narrator, the desperation of the Canaanite woman, the gentleness or surprise of Jesus. Where there is only one character, as found in the discourses of St. John's gospel or in the book of the prophet Isaiah, the lector should try to capture the mood with his voice. He might also try to tip us off, through what he emphasizes, to the focus of the homily.

Interpretive proclamation captures the force and feeling of scripture, not just its sense. Although we are primarily interested in the interpretation and proclamation of scripture, we should also include under this section the dramatic proclamation of extra-biblical readings. These could include a short piece of descriptive prose or a poem by T.S. Eliot like "The Journey of the Magi." Gerard Manley Hopkins also has some excellent poetry that fits a variety of liturgical themes. A couple of examples of his representative poetry would be "God's Grandeur" and "As Kingfishers Catch Fire." All of these and others too can help reinforce or help flesh out in detail the full meaning and impact of a particular piece of scripture or liturgical theme.

2. *Group interpretive proclamations* involve a number of people taking the different parts of a piece of scripture, generally from the gospels. This is something like the reader's theatre. It helps the gospel scene come to life through the rich resource of a number of gifted voices in the congregation. The vocal interpretation sparks our imagination and depicts for us in broad strokes the details of a particular scriptural encounter between God and man.

A suggested model of a group interpretive proclamation is included in this issue. It is the gospel for the twentieth Sunday of the year. It calls for the participation of five to seven voices. The passage deals with Jesus healing the daughter of the Canaanite woman. The character voices would be the narrator, Jesus, the Canaanite woman and at least two disciples.

What advantage does a group interpretive proclamation have over a simple reading? First of all, different voices establish much more easily the presence of different characters. Secondly, the total group effort helps create and lead the congregation in a veritable contemplation of the gospel scene. Although it will take some getting use to, congregations will be much more responsive to these types of proclamations.

Don't be afraid to print up and include parts for the entire congregation. This is certainly encouraged and done at times like Good Friday's proclamation of the Lord's passion. Whenever a piece of scripture calls for a crowd part, a group of scribes or pharisees, townspeople or whatever, involve your congregation. Invite them not just to watch and listen but to participate.

Contemporary plays can also enhance our worship. On special occasions, if a particular scene from a play complements the theme of your celebration, try the group interpretive proclamation technique on it too. Such an opportunity might present itself on the feast of St. Thomas Becket. You might be interested in using a scene from T.S. Eliot's play *Murder in the Cathedral.* If you were celebrating the theme of faith, Paddy Chayefsky's play *Gideon* (based on a real biblical character) has a wealth of material. Archibald MacLeish has another contemporary play dealing with a biblical character. It is entitled *J.B.* It centers around the story of Job. And these are only a few examples of a vast wealth of dramatic literature.

3. A third type of liturgical drama is *mime* or *pantomime.* In this form of drama, a story is generally told without words by means of bodily and facial movements. Marcel Marceau is the most publicized and popular pantomimist in this country. Through mime he creates a complete imaginary world or scene right before our eyes. He proclaims his story through the eloquent communication of his bodily movements and gestures.

There are a number of ways in which mime can be used in liturgy today. To begin with, there is the completely silent mime. Generally, after a reading, a character comes out with a placard which introduces the mime. If your reading was the parable of the prodigal son, your placard might simply read "Father and Sons."

After the mime has been introduced, the players, if not already in position, come in and begin the action of the mime. They use no words, but their meaning, their communication is loud and clear. The mimers can make visible the gospel scene and compound its impact on us.

There is a strange but powerful dynamism in liturgical mime. We are drawn into the scene by the characters. They imaginatively create the whole incident and pull us into the gospel scene not as spectators but participators. Nuances of meaning and feeling are conveyed by the pantomimist in ways simple words could never hope to communicate.

Another way to use mime is with some background music. In this way the music can help you create the mood of the mime. Music is yet another powerful dramatic tool of communication. There is a wealth of music, classical and modern, to help you capture, and create and translate for your congregation feelings of crisis, sadness, melancholy and joy.

Still another form of mime would employ a narrative text. If your theme was "giving" you might enact Shel Silverstein's *The Giving Tree*. One person could narrate the story while two others would mime the parts of the tree and the little boy. This can be used very effectively at both child and adult liturgies. You could use this type of narrative mime with any number of fairy tales that touch on different themes for celebration.

Liturgical mimes are of three types. They can be based on scripture, on extra-biblical readings (e.g., a fairy tale), or they can be "spin-off" mimes. In the first two, the action is somewhat limited and clearly defined by the mime's respective narration (script). The third type does need a word of explanation.

A "spin-off" mime consists of taking the theme, the message or point of a particular piece of scripture, and contemporizing its meaning for a given congregation. Here is an example of what I'm talking about. The scripture scene is Jesus calming the storm at sea. This particular piece of scripture deals with the fear of the disciples, the hostile external environment, Jesus' surprise at his friends' little faith, Jesus' care for them by calming the storm and quieting their fears, and finally the disciples' amazement. We would take any one of these elements and weave a contemporary mime.

How would you go about it? The place to begin is by a group of planners brainstorming. After reading the piece of scripture toss around some questions and ideas. From these the mime will grow. What would be some contemporary storms we find ourselves in? How do we feel abandoned? What are the ways Jesus quiets our fears? How do we know he is present? How does he challenge our faith? It is, at once, a challenge to translate imaginatively the gospel into everyday life situations, as well as an opportunity to proclaim contemporarily that the Word of God is still Good News.

4. *Improvisation* is the next type of liturgical drama. To improvise is to create or invent on the spot. It is taking what is at hand and weaving from it a scenario or story. To use improvisation effectively at liturgy takes much time, work and discipline. The improvisation is actually set when it is done in the context of the liturgy. A group of

planners or players has had the freedom to create and play with an idea or theme long before the liturgy takes place. They have worked with it, refined it, and concretized it. In effect, it has been scripted (set down) by the time it is enacted.

What would be an example of a liturgical improvisation? If your gospel passage dealt with the call of one or a number of the disciples, you might deal with the theme of "calls" in our lives and how we "answer" them. How we respond to everyday calls, demands placed on our time, attention and energy, will give us an idea of how well we can and do respond to the ways the Lord calls us in our lives.

A few years ago a group of fellow Jesuits worked with me on a liturgy I was celebrating that dealt with this theme. The way we approached the improvisation was first to "brainstorm" among ourselves on what were some of the contemporary *Call/Response* situations in our lives. Examining both calls and our actual responses to these calls gave us a wealth of material to work with.

We next began to improvise and play with the different situations until they reached a workable and recognizable form. We found four of the situations we created through improvisation addressed the problem more clearly and eloquently than the others. The four situations, little vignettes, took less than fifteen minutes total time to act out. They consisted of: (1) a young man receiving a phone call he doesn't want to answer; (2) a young hippyish character making some middle class businessmen uncomfortable by asking for some spare change; (3) some early Saturday morning evangelist callers; and (4) a Jesuit community of the future where an obviously troubled young man tries in vain to contact any one of a number of Jesuits through a menacing switchboard. It's football Sunday and the dear fathers are not answering calls.

In each case we represented the unwillingness of individuals to respond to difficult or inconvenient calls. Through the improvisations, each member of the congregation was moved to reflect on all the subtle and less than subtle ways we all fail to respond to the calls in our lives. Through this communal examination of conscience, facilitated by the improvisations, we were moved by the Word of God to confess our negligence in responding to the needs of those around us and seek the renewing strength of the Eucharist in order to better respond to the calls that lay ahead of us.

This would just be one example of what you could do with improvisation. I have found the use of this form of liturgical drama, oftentimes as a homily, to be a powerful and moving experience for a

congregation. It certainly should be used on occasion as a possible liturgical alternative option. But give yourself plenty of time. Make
sure you start long before a liturgy is scheduled so you have time to
create, refine and concretize your improvisations.

5. An adapted form of *psycho-drama,* when used at liturgy, can
prove effective. Psycho-drama is an improvised dramatization. It is
used quite a bit in family or group counseling where tensions and dis-
agreements develop between members. It is designed to allow resolution of conflicts and heightened awareness of the social complexity of
issues for one or more of the participants. The plot is abstracted from
the player's life history.

Now liturgy is not a counseling session. So the way to use
psycho-drama in the context of the liturgy is much along the lines of
an improvisation. Players take the roles of what would be real-life
psycho-drama participants. The developed plot focuses on areas of
conflict for average families, Christians or worshipping groups.

A group of people used this form of drama effectively during a
Lenten liturgy series at the Oakland Cathedral. The theme of the
series was the Ten Commandments. The Sunday that "Honor thy father and mother" was treated, we used some psycho-drama. There
were two players: a father and a son. The father had recently discovered some dope in his son's room. When the son came home, the
father wanted to talk. Actually he wanted to bawl the living daylights
out of him. When the father confronted his son, the son responded
with anger and dismay that the dad would have searched his room.
The two, through yells and screams, proceeded to communicate inef-
fectively with one another.

What the congregation witnessed was a ritual of two wounded
animals. Both father and son felt betrayed. What they wanted to do
was communicate. What neither could see was that their strong feelings of anger and betrayal prevented them from really listening to one
another. They could only strike one another verbally in the way they
felt stricken.

The players never knew when the little drama would end. They
had to act it out, if need be, to its conclusion. But shortly after the
major issues and feelings surfaced, the celebrant rang a bell. Father
and son returned to their respective places. For the homily, the celebrant stood between the father and the son and explained the nature
of reverence: reverence of a son for his father, and of a father for his
son. He developed the suffering and cost of genuine respect and trust.
The very human problems that stand in the way of son-loving father
and father-trusting son. He made the congregation aware of the com-

plexity and difficulty of the fourth commandment.

Father and son flanked the celebrant for the rest of the liturgy. The conflict was still partially unresolved. At the kiss of peace, the celebrant, after a brief exhortation to both father and son about Christian forgiveness, facilitated the reconciliation of the two. Celebrant, father and son then shared this peace with the entire congregation.

6. A sixth type of liturgical drama is what I call the *scenario* or *story dramatization*. This involves the acting out of a short scenario by different characters. This form differs from the group interpretive proclamation. In the group proclamation you simply spark the imagination of your congregation vocally. In the story dramatization all the actor's tools are employed: body and voice.

One type of story drama might be a scene from a play. A full scene might be too long. So it might be a scenic excerpt. If you can find a good translation, or if your congregation would not be put off by Old English, there are countless medieval miracle and morality plays. They could be especially effective during the Christmas, Lent and Easter seasons and other appropriate occasions.

Another possibility would be to resituate a piece of scripture by creating a story dramatization. Take, for instance, the story of the Good Samaritan. Bring it up to date. Who would be a modern parallel to the Samaritan? To the doctor of the law? To the priest? What would be the equivalent of the Road to Jericho? The incident of the New York woman who was stabbed to death in her own front yard while frightened neighbors looked on is a frighteningly similar situation. Human nature is still human nature. Christ still calls us to be involved and we pass him by, wounded on the road, for the very best of reasons.

Try dramatizing a fairy tale or story. There is plenty of literature available. One of Aesop's fables could be done briefly but powerfully. There are many good Sufi stories that lend themselves to dramatization. Idries Shah has edited a number of volumes of them. And Martin Buber has shared a number of excellent Hasidic teaching stories. All are fine material for dramatization.

Perhaps the most challenging type of story dramatization is the one you create and write yourselves. It should be based on some theme you are celebrating. Last year during the Oakland Cathedral's summer series, the Jesuit novices and I were invited to plan the fourth and concluding liturgy on the theme: "Heroes, Sheroes and Other Saints." We got together four weeks before the liturgy and began "brainstorming." The result of this first session was the outline of a scenario we wove eventually into our dramatized story.

Our story included all the basic elements of a hero-story. There were townspeople, a hero who rose from among them, a cantankerous old dragon, a conflict, and a successful resolution. The dramatized story proclaimed, in a most powerful way, that each of us as Christians are called to do battle with the dragons of our lives. The lesson, or what we celebrated, was that God has given us the wherewithal not to kill our dragons—for to rid ourselves of weakness is to divest ourselves of humanity—but to tame them.

7. The final type of liturgical drama is what I like to refer to as *the total dramatic liturgical experience.* Simply put, it is all the possibilities during the celebration of Holy Week that offer themselves for dramatization. Palm Sunday, Holy Thursday, Good Friday and Easter Vigil are all dramatically rich. Each year it is a new challenge to allow some of Holy Week's dramatic richness and evocative power to emerge.

Last year our community utilized a great deal of dramatization on Good Friday. One example of it came in the proclamation of the Passion. Year after year we heard the same gospel proclaimed. This year we decided to mime the Passion. We designed and executed a mime we called "Come Passion" and tried to capture not only the terrible physical suffering and remarkable love found in the Passion, but the personal invitation Jesus makes to each of us to enter into his suffering and dying so we can share the real joy of resurrection.

The dramatic possibilities of Holy Week are many and varied. All you need do is gather a group of imaginative and energetic people. Give yourselves plenty of time. Get in touch with the thematic movement of each day. Then create, refine, concretize and execute.

III. Where can you use it?

You can use liturgical drama in different parts of the liturgy. In the present structure of the Mass, the liturgy of the Word best lends itself to dramatization. The readings and homily are primary moments in the liturgy of the Word. Dramatizations could be effectively used here. Every reading should be at least interpretively proclaimed. However, let me add a word of caution. Using more than one dramatization at a liturgy can diminish its effectiveness as well as overload the liturgy.

Respect the rhythm and movements of the liturgy of the Word and the liturgy of the Eucharist (see Fr. John Mossi's helpful charts in "Liturgical Planning," in Chapter III). Avoid drawing undue attention to parts of the liturgy that are of only secondary importance. Try to heighten and emphasize through dramatization those parts of the liturgy that are of primary importance. Drama is an excellent tool to strengthen and support your liturgical proclamations.

Liturgy planners should not be afraid to explore all liturgical possibilities. If you have a good grasp of where your congregation is, you will not be in danger of pushing them beyond their limits. Remember that a community of worshippers must be led along slowly but surely. The criteria must always be whether what we do helps the congregation celebrate more fully God's saving action in our lives. Certain themes and occasions in the liturgical year demand a more visible and forceful proclamation of this Good News. Dramatizations directed by the right hands and executed by the right bodies and voices can be a valuable tool to accomplish this.

We have only mentioned a few of our potential options. Besides using liturgical drama in the context of the Penance rite, to help proclaim a reading, or as an alternative to the spoken homily, dramatizations might be used in a number of other places. Processions in and out of the church provide excellent opportunities to dramatize.

The eucharistic acclamation offers us yet another opportunity for dramatization. Have you ever tried a non-verbal (dramatized) triple Amen at the conclusion of the eucharistic prayer? At the conclusion of the doxology, as the people are sitting, have them extend their hands palms-up in front of them. This gesture of offering is the first Amen. After a pause, all raise their hands and arms higher in a gesture of even more emphatic offering. This constitutes the second Amen. Finally, after another significant pause, the whole congregation rises and, with hands still palms-up, extends them fully in front of themselves and slightly above the level of their head. This is the concluding Amen. And what you have is a non-verbal dramatization. The effect is powerfully moving.

Still another possibility might be found at the kiss of peace or during the communion meditation. Stretching the imagination even further, what about a non-verbal eucharistic prayer? Difficult? Yes! Impossible? No! All these different moments in the Mass offer themselves for dramatization. It would be good, though, to start with something simple and workable, especially within the context of the liturgy of the word.

IV. Don't Forget

Here are some important guidelines to keep in mind when utilizing drama. Symbols that are not clear are poor symbols at best and probably no symbols at all. Drama that fails to communicate is poor

drama, especially in the context of the liturgy. If you have to explain
it, you've done something wrong.

In selecting and using dramatic forms, ask yourselves the following questions.

1. What is it you want to say? Is it clear in your own mind first?
2. How do you want to say it or proclaim it? (e.g. mime, improvisation, etc.).
3. Is this the best possible way to communicate it? Would a mime be
   better than an improvisation? Or would a group interpretive proclamation be better than a dramatized story?
4. Do you communicate what you want to communicate? *Is it clear?*
5. Do you say it as economically as possible? Do you say no more nor
   less than you want to say? *Is it brief?*
6. Is your communication uncluttered and unencumbered? *Is it simple?*
7. And, as always, the final question and gauge:
   What do people hear you saying? What do they see you doing?
   What is actually communicated?

Planning and using drama in our liturgies involves much hard
work. The results, though, are gratifying. Liturgical drama can help
congregations participate and pray wholly. It is high time we realize
that God's Word is addressed to the whole person, not just his brain
and ear. The more fully we communicate the Good News, the more
powerful this proclamation will be. Rediscovering the dramatic possibilities in our liturgies is simply using all God has given us—body,
voice, heart, mind and spirit—to help his Word become flesh again in
our lives.

Liturgy: A Work of Art?

Doyne Mraz

Dr. Doyne Mraz is a member of Foothill College's Theatre Arts Department. A teacher and director for the College, he also supervises productions for the Palo Alto Community Theatre.

Jean Genet says about the Mass, "Beneath the familiar appearances—a crust of bread—a god is devoured. I know of nothing more theatrically effective than the elevation of the host. . ." Genet's heretical philosophy perhaps earned him the life imprisonment imposed by the French government for breaking laws which are based on Roman Catholic moral precepts. Yet Genet expresses something genuine about the relationship between the human and the Divine. Certainly the Mass brings people together in a single voice and a single affirmation that surpasses the insular condition which Artaud called "art" and transcends into a more general and more significant condition which he called "culture." Unfortunately, the Communion meeting seldom gives the jolt that is expected from a dramatic endeavor.

We may want to look at primitivism to recapture the drama in the Mass. It was from primitive tribal ceremonies in ancient Greece that drama as we know it today was evolved. But primitivism in its pejorative sense carries a connotation of paganism. With our Christian training we hope to avoid paganism of that sort. Yet the early Church Fathers were not afraid to face the reality of the pagan worship influence in the process of the Mass. The Feast of Corpus Christi was created for just that reason. Reflective of our modern Mardi Gras, as seen in New Orleans each year, the Feast of Corpus Christi became a celebration of pagan rites, mummers, dances and uncivilized rituals which the Church not only permitted, but endorsed. I do not wish to infer that we need to go back to those Medieval Dark Ages to find drama in today's Mass. There is a value in the lessons which they taught however. The Gothic cathedrals, no matter how irrelevant to today's world, have their lessons to teach also. Aristotle was most aware of the necessity of spectacle to drama. He listed it as an essential component of all drama. It apparently still remains essential. Today's most viable stage productions are based very strongly upon spectacle: Peter Brooks' production of *Marat/Sade*, the pagan marital tap dancing of George and Martha in *Who's Afraid of Virginia Woolf?* and the most exciting production to hit Broadway in ten years, *Equus*.

It seems to me that when I visit the Mass today, I frequently find a sterile, unserviceable plainness which is reflective of the most barren services exercised by our most conservative Protestant brethren. To avoid being called reactionary, I must say I believe that the English language has helped the Mass in the United States. I also believe there is beauty in sparseness and that a congregation can get a theatrical jolt without being choked by voluminous clouds of incense. I recall a Mass I attended in Oakland. It was conducted by a zealous group of young Jesuits. The entire congregation participated freely and I saw that wonderful production of "culture" which Artaud says is the end of all great creative activity. The pity is that the Mass had been conceived especially for that particular occasion, and while I was told that the home Priest frequently waxed innovative, it was clear that the entire congregation that Sunday had received something special and extraordinary. The point is that the special Mass presentation is occasional and unusual. Most often a congregation faces the same bland transsubstantial food most of the year.

My suggestion is ostensible: the Priest needs theatrical training. He needs more than a nodding acquaintance with dramatic literature and the processes of acting. He needs a full steeping into the aesthetics of the theatre and the processes of creativity. He needs to learn that the Mass is only a blueprint, like any script. The interpretation of the script becomes the *raison d'être* for theatre. No one can do anything more for the Mass, just as no actor can hope to interpret Shakespeare's lines any better than the Bard has written them. The action lies between the lines, and the Priest must learn to create new action between the lines week after week.

Just as sterile as James O'Neill's lifetime of playing *The Count of Monti Cristo* is the sterility of the Mass repeated time after time by a Priest who has only learned one path to style. All great art is created anew each time an audience comes to it. Certainly the liturgy contains enough fresh material to inspire a good actor time after time. Why can't it inspire the clergy?

The Mass seems to be presented two ways: either the congregation may participate fully in all aspects of the theatrical endeavor or it may simply respond to the words of the Priest. There is little doubt in my mind which is favorable. The use of spectacle can create the greatest participation. But we do not need extravagant rose windows, elegant trappings, massive choirs or Michaelangelo's paintings.

A processional might be developed through choric dance. Music need not come from ranks of a great organ. "Play on the cymbal, the tymbal, the lyre." Oral interpretation extends further than a dramatic reading of the commands of Christ. Charles Laughton proved that the New Testament holds narrative gold. The clerical vestments hold infinite possibilities and the green of "after Trinity" can be a multitudinous array of hues. Adolph Appia taught us that theatrical lighting can produce moods and create great emotional effects. All of these things can be combined to show that while the liturgy may be sacrosanct, it need not be static.

Liturgical style extends over the full range of human performance. There are few commitments to the Creed that have not found their voice in a dramatic interpretation which has been cheerfully accepted or noisily rejected. With satire, or with sympathy, by quiet agreement or jaunty disagreement, clerics can open every sort of idea and interpretation to inspection. The resultant revelation of character and conviction is among the particular delights of theatrical liturgy.

The liturgy is a vast composite which makes it a unique art form. Its form works as an aid to understanding the world. Each of the various artists who make it work helps to turn the written and sung word into an experience which approximates life as it is lived and felt moment by moment. Like life, each episode is experienced and then immediately becomes part of the past. Trying to recapture the past is a futile exercise.

The liturgical experience helps one to be sensitive to feelings and ideas, helps one to become aware of his own prejudices and values. In fact, a person may alter opinions when new liturgical experiences and evidences are presented.

In liturgy, as in all art, there is seldom one right answer; there are a number of partial answers, and the final one will probably never be given. A work of art is not a mathematical problem; it adds up in many ways, and at the same time it equals only itself. In some cases, differing opinions cannot all be right; one may preclude another. The best answer lies in the congregation's critical response.

Revitalizing Christian Ritual

William Muller, S.J.

Rev. William Muller, S.J. teaches and directs drama at Loyola High School in Los Angeles.

All Liturgy is ritual and therefore essentially dramatic. Whatever the realities that draw people together to worship, whatever set of symbols people use to articulate their inner faith, the fact remains that some dramatic form will be used to centralize and concretize the common experience. God as unseen and untouchable, faith, hope and even love as unseen and ultimately indescribable challenge us nonetheless to share our common awe and make some meaning from it.

The dramatic art is certainly an attempt to deal with experiences beyond our normal consciousness. The Christian Liturgy of the Eucharist is superb drama, not as was so often thought in the past because of the fancy costumes and expensive props, but because people come around a table to share bread and wine and in the ordinariness of that sharing to discover a reality that makes their ordinariness meaningful. To unmask the hidden, to come face to face with the faceless, to expose the mystery and stand speechless—this is drama, and most especially it is Christian worship.

Most of drama is atmosphere—creating, sometimes manipulating the environment so that only certain sights are seen and only certain sounds are heard. In a conventional theatre the lights shine only on what we are to see and the speakers speak only the sounds we are to hear. This is done to focus our attention and centralize our experience. So it should be in our churches. It has been said that the entrance procession down the main aisle through the congregation symbolizes the election of the priestly ministers from the people of God. It means that, of course, but why not let it be what it more obviously is—a very sure way of getting our attention and using that attention to begin a common and very special experience. From that point on we are confronting the ageless in each of us.

People who come to Mass to be by themselves are in the wrong church. The Eucharist is a public event. It should entertain us, that is, awaken in us memory of all that God has done for us as a people and help us respond to all that God is doing for us now. What God does now, of course, is call us to find out more and more about ourselves together in the Spirit of Jesus, a spirit of justice, compassion and fidelity to the life we have been given. The ritual we engage should be vibrant and totally absorbing—it should say all that we are capable of saying and should make no excuses for the silences we are left with. The speechless moment in theatre is powerful. The speechless moment in Liturgy is the sound of God.

One very important reality in ritual is that there is no audience. We go to the theatre to observe and hopefully to be moved. We go to church all too often to observe and we are happy if we are moved only a little. How sad that we have let our worship become mere observation. To worship is to participate in the ritual. I would go so far as to say that no participation means no worship. Our Christian Liturgy is communal and participatory—anything less is wonderful devotion but certainly not Christian worship. The question now for us is, after all these years of "hearing Mass," what can we do? Everybody prefers to sit and not be bothered. My response is admittedly a bit harsh: pray in your room if you do not like to be bothered in public.

The Roman Rite is rather limiting as a ritual, but there is plenty that can be done to enliven it and make of it a decent, unambiguous liturgical action. The missalettes should be discarded so that people will get in the habit of paying attention to the ritual instead of the commentary. Neighborhood liturgies would help, or perhaps *more* parish liturgies on Saturday and Sunday to create an explicit emphasis on the smaller, more personally involved worship. We need, therefore, priests who are willing to work overtime and be constantly available to the needs of the people. We need a few more priests to be decisive in their parishes, not hesitating between the old ways and the new.

Recorded music is not as involving as live music, but if that's all you can get, then use it. There is nothing wrong with singing along with a record if it will help people participate more fully. Most importantly, though, is the conviction that worship is public, that it is a dramatic and ritual activity—a conviction that when we worship we discover in ourselves and our fellow worshippers that which we can only symbolize.

Symbol is essential to Christian worship. What we see at Mass should challenge us to confront the reality of God. Dirty, dull vestments, colorless and unimaginative church decor, musty or perfumed buildings do not prompt us to "lift our minds and hearts to God." The memorized ramblings and activity of the priest, and the senseless kneeling-sitting-standing of the congregation convince us only that God wants us to be bored. On the other hand, priests engaging the ritual with awe and respect (not sentiment or solemnity) inspire us to join in the special moments we share as a Christian community.

The symbol of the crucifix has been evident in the Church's worship through the ages. I must say I prefer the so-called Protestant cross to the Catholic crucifix. Our primary belief as Christians is that Jesus is alive. The symbol we use, the cross with the body of the dead Jesus hanging on it, tells us certainly that Jesus loved me enough to die for me, but it says nothing about his living for me now. If we keep looking at a dead, limp Jesus, our communal worship life might, little by little, get limp and then die. No wonder our churches are so solemn and lifeless—we seem to be worshiping a dead man. But Jesus is alive, and if we are to ritualize, to make liturgy, to celebrate in his memory, it is his life—his current life—that we must concentrate on. Our worship had better be a joyful experience, celebrating the life of the Man-God who, by dying for us, has shared his new life with us.

Finally, let me say a word about the prayers we say at Mass. The four Eucharistic Prayers approved by the Church are barely adequate. They are poorly written, and they try to express the whole of Christian tradition and insight. Consequently, they speak very little of a specific group of people celebrating a specific occasion. The theatre would have died long ago if those in charge did not put on plays that were well written and that tried to speak to the people's needs while challenging them to fuller consciousness. Our parishes are dying because the service, the worship, the Mass is uninteresting and unimaginative and consequently uninvolving. We are quickly losing our ritual in bordeom. Many new Eucharistic Prayers have been published during the last few years. What we desperately need now is the freedom to use them.

If enough of us are convinced about the need for a revitalization of Christian ritual, Christian ritual will be revitalized. It is really quite as simple as that.

Liturgy and Drama

Judith Royer, C.S.J.

*Sr. Judith Royer, C.S.J., is a member of the faculty at
Loyola-Marymount University. She teaches and directs in
the Theater Arts Department.*

Drama, like literature, must maintain the delicate balance of
word (script), and rite (the translation from the page to the stage).
When this balance is maintained, the theatre-goer experiences the
theatre piece as a total experience: affective, as well as cognitive.
When this balance is disturbed, the theatre-goer may witness an interesting spectacle—ritual without meaning—or a good lecture on life
—word and concept which remain undramatized. While both of these
events may be enjoyable or even valuable, they are not the primary
purpose of the dramatic event any more than they are the purpose of
the liturgical event.

Contemporary dramatists as well as contemporary liturgists
have been concerned with the breakdown of communication through
both word and rite. The proliferation of words as a defense against
communication is a major theme and technique in the works of Eugene Ionesco. T.S. Eliot in *The Cocktail Party* used a very contemporary experience—the cocktail party—as the metaphor for a ritual
celebration which fails either to unite or substantially feed the rich
members of society who gather together for a social function.

Contemporary liturgists have been concerned with the post-
Reformation tendency to substitute the text of the religious service for
the ritual action which should sacramentally express the text. To
paraphrase and somewhat modify the composition teacher's old
stand-by phrase: the contemporary minister too frequently tells them
what he's going to do, tells them what he's doing, and tells them what
he did, instead of allowing the Word of God to become present and
act through the sacramental event as a total religious experience, si-
multaneously affective and cognitive.

One of the most devastating statements about the Void, and contemporary man's terror of the Void in a society where rituals have

171

become empty and meaningless, is Tennessee Williams' expression of his experience of New York cocktail parties.

"Whether or not we admit it to ourselves, we are all haunted by a truly awful sense of impermanence. I have always had a particularly keen sense of this at New York cocktail parties, and perhaps that is why I drink the martinis almost as fast as I can snatch them from the tray. This sense is the febrile thing that hangs in the air. Horror of insincerity, and *not meaning,* overhangs these affairs like the cloud of cigarette smoke and the hectic chatter. This horror is the only thing, almost, that is left unsaid at such functions. All social functions involving a group of people not intimately known to each other are always under this shadow. They are almost always (in an unconscious way) like that last dinner of the condemned: where steak or turkey, whatever the doomed man wants, is served in his cell as a mockingly cruel reminder of what the great-big-little-transitory world had to offer."

Tennessee Williams is just one of many contemporary writers who have experienced and expressed through their works the horror of modern man's isolation within a group. Other modern dramatists —such as the Greek society of the Golden Age, or Western medieval Pinter, Eugene O'Neill, to name only a few—have tried to present the dislocation and sense of fragmentation experienced by modern man in the aftermath of two World Wars and the rise of philosophies of individualism and despair. Some authors offer options for this sense of isolation and despair, others do not. The problem rests in the idea that modern society has lost a sense of common values and common goals which had given members of simpler and more unified societies —such as the Greek society of the Golden Age, or Western medieval and Renaissance societies—a knowledge of their own obligations in that society and a sense of their significance in a larger cosmic scheme of things.

As a teacher of theatre who has also worked with liturgical celebrations over a period of ten years, I have realized a growing tendency among our young people to search for the religious experience in theatre. There seems to be less concern among our theatre students today over "stardom" or success, and greater concern about returning to theatre's original impulses. These were, of their very nature, a religious experience in which man communally confronted the natural mysteries which surrounded him. He found in these natural forces a Power to be dealt with—either by worship, or an attempted control through magic.

In one way I see this as a very healthy tendency in that it expresses a growing demand on the part of our young people to see their lives as meaningful, not only as an isolated existence, but as part of a cosmic scheme which has some universal purpose and meaning. However, I do not believe that the theatre experiences as they exist today should substitute for the need for a religious experience. For Primitive Man, the experience of God and the celebration of His mystery were done directly in relation to the forces of nature. Because of the evolution of religious consciousness and God's intervention into this evolution through the Incarnation and Redemption, Modern Christian Man finds himself incapable of being fully satisfied religiously with a humanistic or naturalistic intercourse with mystery.

The theatre experience—which attempts to balance word and rite —should sensitize man to the mysteries of life, but this should prepare him for participation in the sacramental balance which makes possible the celebration of the Word through ritual communication which Christ and His "new covenant" have made possible.

We cannot expect, however, that either our young people or ourselves can find a full religious and meaningful experience in the liturgical event until we have done some serious examination and re-examination of that liturgical event. If we are providing only lectures about the sacred action which is taking place or surrounding the sacred action with meaningless spectacle, we are failing to let the Word be present and act among us in the communal celebration. In doing so, we move in direct contrast to the Incarnational action of Christ who risked taking on the posture of man—a posture which demands that man maintain a delicate balance suspended between the forces of heaven and the forces of earth, in which Hugo Rahner, S.J., in his book *Man At Play* calls "the heavenly dance."

The Procession

John P. Mossi, S.J.

At the beginning of your average Sunday liturgy, the celebrant, various ministers, and altar assistants have to move somehow from point A to point B. As a unified body, the ministers must navigate from the church vestibule, up the main aisle, and into the sanctuary. Hopefully a procession will create the mood of the celebration. By its pace and symbols a procession sets the stage for what is to come. It can communicate a reverential atmosphere and enable the congregation to enter into the communal prayer of the Church more fully. But, oftentimes processions are sheer chaos. Last-minute preparations, hastily robed celebrants, unclear instructions, ambiguous processional positions, and vague sanctuary stations all add to produce the effect of a Disneyland parade rather than a celebration of the Word of God and the Lord's Meal.

A Visual Statement

Procession is a subtle and very primitive form of religious experience. Theologically, it represents the incarnate Christ walking among his people. Liturgically, the procession, which is a highly visual medium, introduces our major symbols, the Cross and the Word of God, as well as the ministers. The use of music and song during the procession further help to qualify the tone of the celebration.

A little dash of creativity can greatly enhance an entrance. A procession can even hint or announce the theme of the liturgy before any of the readings are proclaimed. For example, a processional banner with a symbolic representation of the seasonal theme or particular celebration can herald a liturgy of reconciliation, a beatitude, a commandment, or a scene from the Gospel. The moving banner follows at a distance of five or six pews behind the cross and acolytes which traditionally lead processions. If several ministers form the procession, one can carry the Lectionary or the Book of the Gospels in an exalted or exposed position. Another minister can carry in the Sacramentary. Remember, however, that the Word of God should occupy a more prominent position than the Sacramentary.

Ministers of Communion, ushers, lectors, cantors, and those who present the gifts on behalf of the community can also be incorporated into the entrance procession at various times. In this way, the procession acknowledges and makes visible the ministries of the total worshipping community.

Models

Diagram A illustrates a procession that can be used on most ordinary Sundays of the year. Can this type of entrance be made a part of your parish worship? How soon?

Diagram B presents a possibility for masses in which a baptism is celebrated. The baptismal party and the liturgical symbols of the rite are highlighted. Perhaps members of the baptismal party can bring in the holy oil, unlit baptismal candle, and white baptismal garment.

Diagram C, a confirmation model, places an emphasis on the sacramental oil, the Word of God, and the fire of the Holy Spirit. The acolytes, which surround the sacramental oil and Word, represent the seven gifts of the Spirit. The use of a processional banner made by the confirmation class would be another way to accent the entrance.

Diagram D is a model for Ash Wednesday. A thurifer with lighted thurible proceeds ahead of the crossbearer and four acolytes. At the center of the nave, the procession stops, permitting the thurifer to incense the cross thereby calling attention to Lent's penitential nature. Similarly, the ashes that will be distributed after the homily also enjoy a solitary position in the procession reminding all to be faithful to the gospel.

There are many ways to creatively enrich the entrance. Centering the procession around a sacrament, special feast, or liturgical season is one way. The readings will offer many possibilities. Study them carefully. For instance, if the concrete image of "salt of the earth" or "light of the world" appears in the gospel, then why not let a glass dish of salt, a lighted candle, and a globe be processed in? These visuals can then become part of the homily.

Processional checklist

1. Make a chart of your church and diagram the procession.
(a) Indicate everyone's place in the procession.
(b) Assign who will carry various liturgical items.
(c) At what point will a bow or genuflection occur?
(d) Indicate everyone's respective sanctuary stations.
2. Practice the procession.
3. Adding more people to a procession does not always produce

a better procession. Insure that each person in the procession has a definite ministry, function, or role in the liturgy.

4. Don't stampede into the sanctuary or process in a tight military formation. A procession needs both a reverential pace and enough space so that the liturgical symbols and the ministers can be seen.

5. Before the procession begins, have the commentator, or appropriate minister, announce the liturgical celebration, the presiding ministers, entrance song, and the fact that the procession is about to commence. The commentator then invites the assembly to stand and face the main doors of the church.

6. Music and song are two very important accompaniments of any procession. They transform an entrance from a dull walk into a festive celebration.

7. Vary the style of your processions. The same type of procession each Sunday quickly lends itself to monotony. One Sunday employ incense, the next a banner, the next the exposed Word of God in raised arm position, the next the processional cross, etc.

8. Adapt the procession to the importance of the Sunday, season, feast, or celebration. The 15th Sunday of the Year is not as important as the Easter procession with the Paschal candle. The four Sundays of Advent are important, but not equally so. Perhaps stress the first which begins the Advent season.

9. Once you have mastered the processional, it is then time to work on the recessional. Use the same principals in leaving the sanctuary as in entering; however, there is one slight change, the pace is slightly quicker.

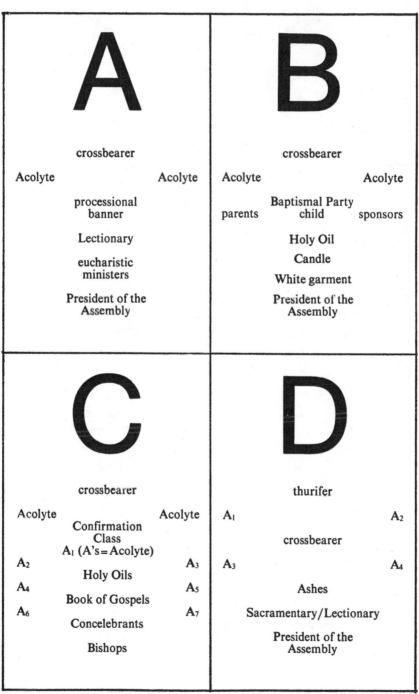

A

crossbearer

Acolyte   Acolyte

processional
banner

Lectionary

eucharistic
ministers

President of the
Assembly

B

crossbearer

Acolyte   Acolyte

Baptismal Party
parents   child   sponsors

Holy Oil

Candle

White garment

President of the
Assembly

C

crossbearer

Acolyte   Acolyte

Confirmation
Class
A_1 (A's = Acolyte)

A_2 A_3

Holy Oils

A_4 A_5

Book of Gospels

A_6 A_7

Concelebrants

Bishops

D

thurifer

A_1 A_2

crossbearer

A_3 A_4

Ashes

Sacramentary/Lectionary

President of the
Assembly

VII
Children's Liturgies

The Need for
Children's Liturgies

William Muller, S.J.

The need for Children's Liturgies is obvious—at least to those of us who live or work with children. Children respond best to sights and sounds that are pleasing and intriguing, and while I suppose we all like bright colors and rich sounds, children rely almost solely on them for meaning. The priest hiding behind the pulpit, dressed in off-white vestments poorly worn, speaking at us about the parish debt is difficult for many mature persons to deal with, but at least we adults can rationalize that the church does need money, that Father Smith doesn't care what he looks like and that he probably had a class once in his seminary days entitled "how to use the pulpit effectively." Meanwhile the fourth graders in the congregation are bored silly and begin acting silly, which is a healthy reaction considering what they are being subjected to. Perhaps we adults should allow ourselves to be bored silly more often; we might insist on some changes for our own worship. Even a fairly organized and challenging adult liturgy is no help to children who are by definition not adult. Why do we continue to expect a fifth grader or even a seventh grader to appreciate the eternal verities when parents, teachers and priests cannot adequately explain them? And the problem is mostly this: much of Christianity is in the living of it, not in its analysis. Children cannot live as adults, and so it is obvious that their Christianity and their expression in worship should be that of children.

I was present at two first communions recently. The family affairs were warm, friendly and filled with real Christian joy, while the liturgical affairs were ludicrous. The church doings were cold, impersonal and only remotely were they celebrations. One of the readings used at one liturgy was from the Acts of the Apostles exhorting Christians to stay away from strangled meat and fornication. A seven year old (boy or girl) being told not to fornicate is nothing short of dangerous, and how long has it been since you've eaten strangled meat? At the other liturgy the children were so well choreographed and disciplined they looked like robots sitting and standing and answering in unison at all the prearranged cues. The children seemed to

be self-motivated, that is to say there were no nuns to be seen anywhere near the children, but I soon discovered the leader nun clicking
her infernal clicker at which noise the first communicants jumped,
squealed and tried to smile. I think they really did want to smile but
were afraid to.

We have all been to churches where the priest has raised his
voice (yelled) at a poor mother or father because little Johnny pre-
schooler wants to know what's going on. We have all witnessed the so-
called Children's Mass on Sunday morning and most of us remember
it from our past. The single memory I have of the Children's Mass of
my youth (St. Raymond's, 9 A.M.) is fear. Nobody can talk me out of
my memory of fear either, since it is corroborated by other memo-
ries: parents promising our favorite breakfast as a reward for enduring the Sunday ritual, for instance. I say ritual because it certainly
was that. The middle-aged priest talking like a pal (or buddy or friend
or father or God depending on his mood), we kids prompted by
parents to say thank you to Father after Mass, and Father laughing
with our parents about how cute we all were and, of course, how well
behaved.

Most teenagers are insulted to be called children, but they are
not adults so I include them here as post-children, or not-quite-adults,
or, as a colleague calls them, pre-human. No matter what we call
them, they have a need to live their faith and worship as teenagers,
not as adults. I teach at a Jesuit high school and the liturgy plays a
special part of what we try to do for our students. However, what
should have been the two most significant liturgies of the year—the
Mass of the Holy Spirit at the start of the school year and the Graduation Mass—were not that well prepared nor were they executed
(prayed) with much concern for the congregation. The homily at the
Graduation Mass turned into a sermon (two or three sermons, actually) and was at least thirty feet over the graduates' heads. What saved
the liturgy was the music which the graduates liked and the adults
didn't like, of course. What strikes us adults as important and valuable for all eternity may not strike our teenagers that way. They almost necessarily reject what is forced on them, and while this may
not be the best for them or us, it is the current state of affairs. What
we should be doing for our teenagers is providing them opportunities
to discover and articulate their values and share them with others. We
should be challenging them to grow up their own way and not be
forcing them to grow up our way.

The impression I have created, I'm afraid, is that I want better
homilies for children and teens. I want that, but I want much more.

The whole liturgical experience has to be reformulated. A penance rite for pre-schoolers is ridiculous. Elementary school children reciting the creed, which is an intelligent doctrinal statement intended for adults, is a waste of time. Teenagers subjected to a series of prayers that say nothing to them or about them, will leave the Church for who knows what.

Hopefully, all of us in the Church can agree on this much at least, that we are a community of persons of all ages who believe in and confess the Lord Jesus as the Son of God, the Savior of mankind. What meaning our belief brings to our daily lives is rather personal, but will be shared in the common worship we participate in. A liturgical structure to provide for the needs of the various segments in a parish is crucial and must include a liturgy or liturgies for children.

The Children's Mass should be conducted anywhere but in the church itself. A very simple parish hall can be transformed easily into a bright, warm liturgical place for children. Pre-schoolers should have their own "bible study" perhaps, as well as supervised playtime (baby-sitting). First, second, and third graders should have their own Liturgy of the Word, telling and acting out Bible stories, making posters and vestments. A liturgy of the Word for the fourth to seventh graders should center on their discovery of themselves as persons, persons loved by God; persons responding somehow to the God in their lives. They, too, can act out Bible stories, make things for the Eucharistic Celebration, and hopefully begin to build a rational Christian response. Obviously, seventh graders are not adults and cannot be expected to respond as maturely as they will in time, but beginnings must be made even with ones so young. A healthy attitude toward sin and penance, for instance, can be the fruit of a series of Children's Liturgies. Proper understandings of tradition, authority, reverence, and so forth, must begin early or our children will grow up with more problems than we grew up with (if that's possible). They already have misconceptions, which are inevitable, I guess, but these can be found out and cleared up with the help of a liturgical structure for children.

Recently I celebrated a Children's Liturgy and after a single Bible reading (I always use a story) and a few choice words, I asked the children (third and fourth graders) if they had any questions. Did they have questions! "What's the red stuff you put into the cup?" "Why doesn't Jesus taste better?" "What color is God?" There are always questions with children, and I found the Liturgy of the Word a very appropriate opportunity to answer those questions and talk about God and how children respond to God.

If two groups are formed for two separate Liturgies of the Word, most of the time the groups should join together for the Liturgy of the Eucharist. The Eucharist is the central worship of the community and should be prayed as a community. Occasionally it might be nice to have a smaller Eucharistic Celebration with only fourth and fifth graders, say, while the rest of the children are together for their Eucharist. Needless to say, the Eucharistic prayers must be suited to children. The new Eucharistic Prayers for Children are ideal in this regard. It is very important that the children have some part in the prayer saying. Children are as bad at listening as we are, so give them some of the prayers to say throughout the liturgy. And it is important, certainly for the younger ones, that the Eucharistic Prayers be the same or at least similar for a number of weeks in a row. Be sure to have plenty of music that the children know and can sing. If they don't know much at the start, then teach them one or two songs and use those songs over and over, adding a new song or two every couple of weeks. The table (altar) should be low to the ground, since everyone knows children prefer sitting on the floor to sitting on chairs. Let the children get as close to the table as possible. Closeness and familiarity will breed not contempt, but understanding and healthy response. We can do well to save the mystery and awe of it all till they are older. Better to have children grow into reverence because they know what's going on, than be forced to reverence over what they think is magic. Christianity is sometimes strange, but never magic.

A Children's Liturgy demands a hardworking and imaginative group of adults to plan, organize, supervise, and execute. They must devote themselves to the task for at least a six month period—ten or twelve people "trading off" Sundays won't work. Consistency and repetition are primary values when working with children. The priest for the celebration should be the same priest every week for a period of weeks. It is not necessary that the priest be newly ordained or even young. I know an eighty year old pastor who gets along better with children than his brand new assistant. Whatever the age of the priest, he must be comfortable with children, be able to be genuinely friendly with them, and not be condescending or preachy. Warmth and personality are helpful, as are story telling and clowning ability. But most important of all is the conviction that children need their own liturgy, that the faith so dear to us must be passed on to our little ones honestly, openly, and with great concern for them.

It is not necessary to "do everything" at every liturgy. Children, like adults, deal better with one idea at a time, so plan accordingly. If the theme of the liturgy is peace, then, there is no reason to clutter the liturgy with other ideas, even though they may be related in our adult minds. Perhaps the penance rite would be dropped altogether, along with the presentation of gifts. Obviously the Kiss of Peace would be highlighted and might be placed after a simple reading and talk about Jesus as peacemaker and how we have to be peaceful. With older children, perhaps a discussion homily about war and peace might be productive. At any rate, keep Children's Liturgies simple and to the one point.

Someone complained to me recently that every Mass he has ever gone to has been a recounting of the history of salvation and a plea for money. If we can give our children variety, and little by little over the years give them a straightforward, magic free vision of our Christian faith, with financial concerns in the background, as they grow older they will discover for themselves the newness and richness and wonder of our Christian worship. By the time today's children are adults, perhaps the adult liturgy will be more challenging and responsive to their needs. We must start now with our children.

Lastly, let me tell you what great fun it is to work with children, especially in teaching them to pray. Kids do not worry about adult problems, and while they certainly have problems of their own, they give them up very quickly when engaged in stimulating activity. The joy and sheer wonder of an eight year old, the wisdom of an eleven year old, and the determined searching of a teenager are infectious. I learn more about Christianity working with and for these young people than I learned in most classrooms. I am constantly being challenged by children, challenged to practice what I preach and to preach only what is truth, justice, compassion and fidelity to the goodness God has given each of us. Those who work with children have been kept honest, filled with life and eagerness to serve. Where would we be without children? Even Jesus knew what graces and joys there are to be found with children: "Bring the little children to me, and become like them yourselves to enter the kingdom of heaven."

Liturgy with Children

James Notebaart

I. A Review of the New Directory

The Church recently issued a *Directory for Masses with Children*. This document marks another step in liturgical reform because it draws on the concept of adaptation. The concept of adaptation was reborn when Vatican Council II said that authentic variations are valuable and even to be fostered. The document points out that liturgy is often an adult event and that the level of meaning for adults is different than for children. Yet it affirms that the center of worship lies in its *meaning* for those celebrating it. So the movement is a logical one from adapting adult liturgies to adapting liturgy for children.

The *Directory* says that liturgy has an impact upon children. That impact should bring religious experience, rather than spiritual harm. Children must understand the liturgy. In order to understand liturgy, they must have a foundation which gives both the human dynamic as well as the spiritual. The two are to work together. Sentiments of friendship, gratitude, and festivity are to be bound to Christian values.

We have to ask ourselves where this foundation comes from. The *Directory* points in several directions. Parents are seen as the first teachers, in humanity and in faith. The Christian community, secondly, has a role of teaching children the Gospel values, the love that Christians have for one another and involvement in authentic prayer.

A further instrument in teaching children is liturgy itself. This teaching experience happens as the children are instructed by God's word and as they share the Gospel values of love in communion. The *Directory* says: "clearly accommodated to the age and mentality of the children, it should attempt, through the principal rites and prayers to convey the meaning of the Mass, including a participation in the whole life of the Church."

It is important to note that the liturgical experience is explained in the context of variety. Variety is essential for children because repeated exposure to the same adult experience can dull the senses of a child rather than create growth. The *Directory* is careful to note, however, that liturgy should not be too didactic. The Eucharist is not

186

to be celebrated if the children can not learn from it, or if they are not able to experience it as their prayer. A word service would be more appropriate in this case. If the children are at a Sunday liturgy, a separate word service might be appropriate as well.

The *Directory* then moves beyond the liturgy as a teaching device and places its focus on better celebration for children. It cites the tension which exists when adults are present, because then the liturgy must speak on several levels at once. Yet it says that children should be involved as much as they can be at these times. This involvement should lead to active and conscious participation.

The character of the liturgy should be one which takes into account all the various roles of the liturgy (readers, cantors, preachers) so that there is no monotony. The liturgy is to have an atmosphere that is festive, fraternal, and prayerful. Liturgy for children must be alive to children. It must be a celebration as children understand festivity. They should know that the priest is interested in them and wants to pray with them, and they should be led to a sense of prayer in which God is in their midst.

There are a number of factors which determine this experience of festivity and prayerfulness. The place and time of the celebration should be determined according to the children's attention span and suitability. How the children experience a space is likewise important in determining where to pray. The type of decoration present is to be given great prominence.

The singing, musical instruments, etc. should be appropriate and simple. The children should have a real sense of being part of the music making. The *Directory* even says that reproduced music, such as tape recordings, may be appropriate. Complementing music, silence is seen as a real part of children's experience. Parents often wonder if their children can ever be quiet. Yet the *Directory* does ask for prayer, not pandemonium. In suggesting silence, it has an overactive liturgical style in mind. Some contemplation is called for on the children's part. So a balance is sought between pure activity, and "dry and merely intellectual" liturgies.

In general the parts of the Mass may be simplified, although care should be taken that there is some continuity with the general liturgy. The introductory rites should create an "assembly in unity" and then prepare for hearing the Word. The Word service should not be unduly long, and it should be clear to the children. Use of children's Bibles is possible, but they should be accepted by a competent authority. The prayers of the leader may be adapted to fit the children. These prayers should not be moralizing (e.g., "I told you what would happen if you disobeyed"), nor should there be baby talk (e.g., "Baby Jesis, I lob ya berry berry mush"). What is asked for is a consistent style of prayer that is appropriate, meaningful, and involving. This same sense is asked in the Eucharistic prayer, although for the time being one of the four approved versions is to be used. Work is now being done on children's Canons.

The document concludes with a beautiful summary:

> "The contents of the directory are intended to help children quickly and joyfully to encounter Christ together in the Eucharistic celebration and to stand in the presence of the Father with him. If they are formed by conscious and active participation in the Eucharistic sacrifice and meal, they should learn day by day, at home and away from home, to proclaim Christ to others among their family and among their peers, by living the 'faith, which expresses itself through love'" (Galatians 5:6).

II. General Observations

One fact is very clear in the whole tone of the *Directory:* liturgy for children is really *their* prayer. We are to view it in terms of *their* ability to participate and understand worship. Imposing adult elements may be wrong. We can not risk spiritual harm in the lives of children. It is important then that we should know the children with whom we celebrate. We should learn as well their various educational and experiential levels. The following is a sketch which may help in understanding grade level abilities.

First grade

One of the most challenging tasks is to celebrate in a truly childlike frame of mind. Most often we try to water down our theology, and it comes off as watered down theology. What we should do is understand their thinking and speak to them as adults. We don't have to become children to think in their patterns. This is critical at the first grade level. If you fake interest, they will know. The first grader has a very short attention span at the beginning of the day and at the beginning of the year. Five or ten minutes might be all the time you have. It is short at the end of the day as well. Take advantage of the time from 10:00-11:30 A.M. Gradually during the year you can lengthen your prayer time.

When you are calling children to prayer, let them know what you are going to do. Tell them firmly if they misbehave. The leader of prayer has a great control over their attention and behavior.

The styles of prayer are varied. The sense of touch will play an important part so liturgies can be quite tactile. At this age children will want to act things out, but they will need a lot of direction from the leader. Children at this age are just beginning to understand rhythm and beat and tone.

Topics of prayer are frequently family, hurting, helping, being a brother or sister.

Many of these themes can be brought out by stories that are told by the leader or by the children themselves. Kids respond well if they feel they are part of the prayer. They like to repeat prayers. The litany form can be valuable for them.

Second grade

In many respects second graders are similar to first graders. Their attention span is somewhat longer. They tend to be more mature, or at least they think of themselves as more mature. Group acting is more coordinated and the children need less direction. The liturgies are pre-Eucharistic forms of sharing. The meal can be a great source of prayer for the children. Parallels in birthday celebrations, seasonal days, etc. focus on the Eucharist.

Third grade

If the children receive communion in either second or third grade, decisions about liturgy are key. One wants the liturgies to move from the ordinary celebrations of togetherness to a more formal sense of the ritual of Mass. One important factor to understand is the relation between adult liturgy and children's experience of that liturgy. The children may understand the participation elements better than they do the verbal thrust. So capitalize on what they are to *do* in liturgy. One grade I know grew the wheat and made their own bread for the Eucharist.

Fourth grade

A fourth grader feels that he is pretty much an adult and sometimes he doesn't like all that kid stuff he did the year before.

The sense of touch means holding hands with girls and that is so unboyish. Yet while they separate themselves from the past grades they are often still very much children.

Participation in planning becomes important because fourth graders really will speak their preferences. Sometimes long term projects can culminate in a liturgy. These can be either study projects or craft projects. Topical liturgies work quite well.

Fifth and Sixth grades

Fifth and sixth grades are demarcation lines in the children's lives. For now they are becoming aware of the whole world with its problems and its people. If they ask to have a fast for those who are starving, they mean it. If they sponsor a collection for those in need, it is because they are becoming aware of suffering.

At this time the relationship they have with the leader of prayer is critical. They should know him and they should feel comfortable with him. At this time as well they are becoming more aware of the changes within them. There are many things that will embarrass them.

Seventh and Eighth grades

Sometimes these grades are very sentimental, the type of liturgy they like is a bit on the soggy side. Answering their liturgical needs is very difficult, because you want to lead them toward good liturgy. One day you can have communion under both species and they will act like adults, and at another time you can have it and they will act like three year olds. You set the mood, you control the situation, yet they want to be part of the planning. At this age level your liturgies cannot succeed unless they have a hand in it. For they are trying to understand how they believe and what their belief means in daily life.

Death and Children

It is very difficult to deal with the peers of a deceased child. Children see death as foreign. They are frightened, and yet they want to do what they can. Sometimes at this point holding and supporting them is all you can do. When death happens, this is the main religious question for the rest of the year, especially at an older age. You can do a lot by bringing them through the mourning period in a personal and a liturgical way.

Children have the capacity to do many more things than adults. A second grader would be happy to be an oar, or one of the waves, or Jesus. They truly can feel what it is like to be a boat tossed then calmed by the Lord. Children have a broad and uninhibited imagination. To sing and dance and act are part of their being. To children belong the visions of Christianity; they can see the future in ways that are more pure and simple and more real than adults beset with practical matters. Like children, Jesus and the apostles saw the Kingdom of the Father and believed it could come about. If children can still see this same kingdom, how can adults take this vision away from them? To be visionary and to allow all parts of our lives to fill liturgy is a requirement for children's liturgy. The seasons have an effect on children. Snow in their faces, cold birds huddling around a warm air vent, say more to children than we allow to be said to us. Stories become real and fantasy can make Christ present.

Liturgy can happen as prayer and play, as dancing and as vision. It can happen directly and quickly or more formally in Church. We must be sensitive to prayer as it happens, and we must be able to sense the presence of Christ in our midst.

A Season of Surprise

Sr. Patricia Helin

Sr. Helin is principal of the Santa Theresa School of Religion in San Jose, California. She has worked for many years with children's liturgy.

Advent, by its very nature and position within the liturgical calendar, offers an opportunity to reawaken within the minds and hearts of children the awareness of Jesus' coming. Despite the commercial emphasis so prevalent within our society, the awe and wonder inherent in the Christmas mysteries can still outweigh the Santa Claus-Mistletoe aspect of the days between Thanksgiving and December 25. What has been heard and explained any number of times can be new and exciting, especially if the wonder of the reality can be retained and communicated to those eager ears always ripe for storytelling. Advent is the time for storytelling. Maybe in the past we neglected to tell the *whole* story. Maybe we eliminated the essential element for understanding a story so profound—the attitude of a prepared heart.

The story of Christ's birth, despite its scriptural simplicity, contains elements of deep meditation. With proper guidance, even the very young can enter into the investigation. The story of Jesus had a beginning—Christmas—but its only ending is that which each Christian gives to it by his or her life. During this season of reawakening, how can we revitalize the story of Jesus in the lives of those we try to inspire?

Ideally, the place for all teaching is the Sunday Eucharistic Celebration. During this time the Christian family can listen together to the mysteries of faith, and rekindle dead or dying sparks of light and truth. The liturgical readings selected for the season of Advent re-emphasize the marvels of God becoming-one-with-us, but without proper planning and careful creative expression, they can be dismissed easily and readily as monotonous jargon. Appropriately, the homily time should incorporate a learning experience for all, either visually, experientially, or dramatically. Advent lends itself to all three of these expressions. With planning, Advent can make Christmas a time of spiritual rebirth for all. However, if meaningful, pedogogical liturgy is unavailable to the Sunday celebrative community, the young of the parish could be gathered together during the designated education time to prepare for the Sunday Eucharist. The following suggestions could be implemented either in a large group, hearing the Word of God in para-liturgy, or within the individual classroom as a scripture study. Whatever method is selected as best suited for the local parish situation, it is always expedient to reflect upon the purpose for such a celebration. We strive to bring to a greater awareness within each child that Jesus was sent by the Father to bring us a great surprise, the gift of new life. Our life is now a part of His Life, and every Advent prepares us to receive that gift again and again. The gift given and received on that first Christmas is a daily occurrence, if we can be alert to the signs of His presence.

The Sunday readings for Advent 1974 have been taken from the "A" cycle of the New Lectionary. Even though the first and second readings are rich in imagery and theology, they might require more scriptural investigation than the parish teacher has time to undertake in order to interpret them properly and in context. However, they have been selected purposely and should be read and thought about in conjunction with the Gospel. Children in grades six, seven and eight enjoy research work and could contribute some new insights into these Old Testament and Apostolic writings by using a biblical commentary or bible dictionary in their class during this season. I have drawn from the selected Gospels of the "A" cycle in establishing the four themes of the Advent season. I see each describing an aspect of the chosen seasonal theme of SURPRISE.

First Sunday of Advent——**Watch**
Second Sunday of Advent—**Prepare**
Third Sunday of Advent——**Believe**
Fourth Sunday of Advent—**Dream**

This thematic approach to teaching is a unifying and direct methodology that allows for intense study as well as free association. I suggest using this method with children especially because of its experiential qualities. What child, or even adult, does not enter imaginatively and enthusiastically into the world of *Surprise*? Truly, the Father's love expressed in Jesus was and still is a *surprise* to mankind. Advent directs our attention to the reality of that love and allows us to ponder it anew, making its dynamism an integral part of our everyday lives. Advent says: *Watch! Prepare! Believe! Dream!* Do we?

The following outline offers a basic plan for creating a "liturgy-lesson" around the proposed Advent themes. The material can be extended to include the entire class time (usually one hour) or be abbreviated in order to supplement the assigned lesson. Each lesson should precede the Sunday celebration which might necessitate combining two lessons if vacation interferes.

Seasonal Theme: SURPRISE
Weekly Themes: First Sunday —*Watch*
　　　　　　　　　Second Sunday–*Prepare*
　　　　　　　　　Third Sunday —*Believe*
　　　　　　　　　Fourth Sunday–*Dream*
— What does the word connote on a natural level?
— What associations do we make with this word?
— People?
— Things?
— Places?
What experiences can you share?
(Relating your own personal experiences in a story form is always a meaningful and interesting method used to initiate discussion.)

Listening to the word of God:
　　At this time share the Sunday Gospel by reading the selection from the Bible that has been given a place of honor in the class area. Prepare the children to listen to the reading, keeping in mind the theme just discussed. (Allow a minute or two of silence so that each child can be aware of a special message from God through His Word.)

Share:
　　　　— What did the reading say to us?
　　　　— What does it say about Jesus' coming?
　　　　— What does it tell us to do?
　　　　— What pictures do we see in our minds while listening?
(Re-emphasize the selected theme word and make the associations between the theme and the reading.)

From the children's suggestions choose symbols that will demonstrate their understanding of the theme. This will vary with the age level.
These symbols can be drawn, cut and attached to the banner in the area for the week's theme.

Creative project:
　　In order to communicate the integration of each week's lesson to the whole of the Advent season, I suggest choosing one project

that will extend over the four weeks to be shared by the entire school or parish in some way.

Suggestions:

— *A Growing Banner or Collage*

— *A Mobile*

— *A Homemade Slide Show (using commercial slides or those made by using contact paper) This slide show can be shared with the entire religious education program at the last class before Christmas.*

Closing:

A song appropriate for the theme and one likely to be included in the Sunday celebration. Some suggestions might be.

Watch:

The King of Glory
My Sweet Lord
My Soul Is Longing for Your Peace
Open Your Eyes
Day by Day
We Long for You, O Lord

Prepare:

Prepare Ye the Way of the Lord
O Come, O Come Emmanuel
The Coming of Our God
Prepare For the Coming of the Lord
Song of Good News

Believe:

Put Your Hand in the Hand
Go Tell It On the Mountain
And I Will Follow
Keep in Mind
Sing Out, My Soul

Dream:

Lord of the Dance
Last Night I Had the Strangest Dream
We Shall Overcome
Blowing in the Wind
If I Had a Hammer
Day is Done
Get Together

Since our level of understanding and knowledge is dependent upon our sensory involvement in any learning process, it is only fitting that we consider teaching the Christian message with the same approach. One visual that can be incorporated into the learning experience is a project of banner making which grows with each week's lesson. It. is an excellent source of review, as well as a meaningful expression of the children's understanding of scriptural truths communicated via sign and symbol. Its size, and the quality of materials used to create it, can vary depending upon the number of children involved, their age level, and the budget allowance for such activities. Knowing that it will be hung in the church during the Christmas season should be sufficient motivation to make it aesthetically attractive. In one parish, such a banner was created by a class of junior high students and utilized at Sunday liturgy each week during Advent to visually demonstrate the meaning of the Sunday homily. For many parents it was an insight into the depth of religious understanding in their young children. In some cases this understanding was more developed than their own.

Hopefully, this method of instruction will also reinforce the integration that is needed between liturgy and formal religious instruction. The suggested approach is only one method out of many by which the richness of the liturgy can be incorporated into a classroom experience, so that the classroom learning can be meaningfully expressed in liturgy. Hand in hand they will unfold the story of Advent and the whole liturgical year—God's love is so great that He gives His only Son to dwell with man!

Let's Play a Prayer

Sr. Patricia Helin and Susanne S. Mallory

Susanne S. Mallory is a free-lance writer, who has been active in planning liturgies for many years.

In addressing ourselves to the subject of children's liturgies, we are confronted with a basic dilemma. We assume that the only kind of worship experience that makes sense for the young is one in which they feel relaxed, comfortable and thoroughly themselves. Children at prayer should not be too different from children at play. The element of doing things to please adults, or to conform to certain rules adults have fixed, is not what one would call a desirable component of a children's liturgy. Yet, on the other hand, these specific times set aside for prayer should not be meaningless in their makeup. Children should sense that what the group is doing together is enjoyable and meaningful to everyone participating. To approach this subject of liturgy or religious experience from their perspective, we have to ask ourselves the question: "What is a child's world like?"

Child psychologists tell us that play is the child's natural medium of self expression, the way he knows himself and lets himself be known. Play is not only amusement, but also a means of gathering information about the world around him. Play itself includes the same key elements found in liturgical worship: storytelling, music, song and rhythmic movement, visual arts and drama. Each of these elements should be carefully chosen to achieve a liturgy appropriate to the age of the children and to the occasion being celebrated. We hope this article will help you better understand the why, when, where and how of children's celebrations.

Psychology gives us the reasoning, the *why*, behind children's liturgies. "We may fear spiritual harm if over the years children repeatedly experience in the church things that are scarcely comprehensible to them: recent psychological study has established how profoundly children are formed by the religious experience of infancy and early childhood, according to their individual religious capacity." This quote was taken from *The Directory for Masses with Children*

197

issued December 1973. Liturgy can be both an outlet for past experiences and an opportunity for new experiences.

A key word in children's liturgies is celebration. Just what does celebration mean to children? To them, it is externalizing an interior feeling of joy and happiness on a special occasion. Halloween, St. Valentine's Day, Fourth of July, Christmas, Easter and birthdays are probably the ones which children celebrate best. These are fun, enjoyable times. Times of giving and receiving, times of song and festivities, and of reunions with family and friends. These "celebration" times can guide us to the *when* of children's liturgies. Any of the aforementioned holidays, other National and Liturgical holidays and seasons, and Mother's and Father's Day all provide special occasions for special liturgies. The analogy of God, our Father, to our earthly fathers can be strongly made on Father's Day. We can transfer the concept of celebration children have to the Eucharistic celebration if we present it as an occasion to share a meal with people we love, to reaffirm our belief in God, and to have happy reunions with friends.

Children's liturgies need not always be celebrated in church according to the new *Directory for Masses with Children*. When contemplating *where* to hold a liturgical celebration, analysis of the group and the purpose or theme of the service are important. Certain pertinent questions should be asked by those responsible for planning and preparing the liturgy. Will this be a whole-parish liturgy, a grade or age-level grouping, or a special *families* gathering? Sometimes the age level of the group and its size may lend itself to other than a church setting. Consider the lawn for a spring time, new-life celebration; a home for CCD class or intimate *family* group; a backyard or wooded grotto area, even the beach, can be an appropriate place to celebrate the magnificence of God's creation. Perhaps the Liturgy of the Word could be celebrated nearby before bringing the children into the main body of the church for the Liturgy of the Eucharist. One successful Easter celebration had the pre-school children enjoying an Easter Egg hunt outside on the church grounds with teens supervising, while the rest of the parishioners were participating in the Liturgy of the Word. All celebrated the Liturgy of the Eucharist together.

The *how* of children's liturgies has been briefly mentioned when we stated that play includes key elements of liturgical worship: storytelling, music, song and rhythmic movement, visual art and drama. Verbal involvement, other than singing, is also important.

Storytelling has its place in the Liturgy of the Word. Many of our adult readings without storytelling have little meaning to young minds. There are many sources of children's literature which can be substituted for the epistles. Books we have employed for liturgical usage include *Velveteen Rabbit, Nog's Dream, A Fuzzy Tale,* and *The Little Prince* as well as *Jonathan Livingston Seagull, The Giving Tree, Hope for the Flowers,* and *The Red Balloon.*

Music, song and rhythmic movement mean involvement, but involvement means not only active participation, but also meditative listening to instrumentation or solo or group renditions. Guitar is most often associated with children's liturgies; organ and various band or orchestra instruments can also be used along with tambourine and even handmade music makers. Rhythmic movement can incorporate dance and gesture. The purpose of these can be the expression of self through very creative means. To be done well, however, dance does need professional people guiding, advising and participating. Gesture can be as simple as a friendly hug at the sign of peace, upraised hands at the Offertory, or as complex as rhythmic waving of arms in unison at an Alleluia. Other actions which the children might participate in are processions—entrance, offertory, communion and recessional.

Visual art can be used to depict the theme of the particular liturgy. Banners are the most-often-thought-of visuals. Others include a Blessings Tree, a Jesse Tree, placques, and posters. Use of opaque or overhead projectors can help illustrate a reading or a homily. Slides or a film can effectively be used in place of a reading or precede or enrich a dialogue homily. Various props also can be utilized: balloons —helium filled for Pentecost to depict Spirit; kites with a Christian message on each and tacked high on the walls; and large paper flowers made by the children themselves. On one occasion, the newly confirmed shared their gifts of the Spirit with the worshipping community by distributing paper flames with a gift of the Spirit written inside. Each member of the congregation renewed his confirmation commitment and reflected on how his particular "gift" had been lived since.

Drama immediately brings to mind Christmas pageants, but consider if you will drama or pantomime with readings. Children in our parish have successfully pantomimed *The Giving Tree* to transmit a message during the Liturgy of the Word on Holy Thursday. The story was selected as illustrating the total-giving of Jesus and the total-giving of a real Christian. It is advisable to practice many times with the children beforehand to assure seriousness and confidence during the performance.

By verbal involvement, not only singing is meant, but also performance of the usual lay-adult functions of lectoring and helping to write select prayers such as The Creed and the petitions of the faithful. A child can effectively give the homily at a First Communion Mass and several of the confirmandi might give their testimony and witness to their new commitments to Jesus.

Careful study and prayer-filled investigation should precede the planning of any liturgy, but especially a liturgical celebration involving children. Liturgy should prepare the children to receive the Word of God and the power of the Spirit as it unfolds in their lives by celebrating their lives prayfully and playfully.

What Do You See?

Sr. Margaret Ehlen

*Sr. Ehlen is Director of St. Leo's Religious Education
Center in Oakland, California. She has several years of experience in working with children, and for the past three
years has worked with a new experimental program at St.
Leo's.*

Introduction

Note: *Direct the children to keep their eyes closed until they
know what to look for, and to imagine what the things look like even
before they look for them.*

Eyes are fantastic things. We can close them to see nothing.
Then we can open them to see almost anything we want to see. Let's
close them. Now open them to look at as many people in the room as
we can see. Now close them. Now open them to see where the light is
coming from. Look at the lights and the windows. Now close them.
Now open them to look at all the things colored brown you can see.
Now close them. Now open them to look at all the round things you
can see. Now close them. Now open them to look at all the smiles
you can see.

Remember all the things we saw? Remember what it's like to see
something for the first time? Sight is a special gift. Let's sing a song
about seeing. Song: *What Do You See* by Betsy Chapman.

Penance Rite

*Use a television set. Have the room darkened and turn the ma-
chine on, but to a blank picture with light only.*

Now as we come to the part of the liturgy where we say we are
sorry for things we have done to hurt others, let's see ourselves. As I
turn on the TV, imagine yourself on the screen. It is a time this past
week when you did something you are not very happy about. It was
something you would do very differently now if you had it to do over.
Look at the screen and watch yourself.

Now I'm going to change the channel. It's another blank channel, but this time you see yourself differently. You see yourself in the same situation, but this time you are acting differently, the way you would want to act. Watch yourself again.

Now as I turn off the TV, go to the picture inside yourself. Talk to the Jesus in you and make a promise to try to be on the second channel this week.

Let's close with our Act of Contrition *(use an overhead projector in same darkened room):*

O my God I have sinned
I am sorry. Please forgive me.
I disobeyed you and hurt others.
I deserve to be punished.
But I know you love me,
and I want to love you more.
With Jesus' help
I will try to make up for my sins,
and stay away from all
that leads me to sin. Amen.

First Seeing
   Begin to light candles. Have parents or helpers situated around the room, and signal them to light the candles. Use background reading or music during the quiet, such as I am the Light of the World *by John Fisher.*

The room has been dark, but now it is becoming light as we see candles being lit all around us. It's a good feeling to be able to see, and especially to see candles and candle flames. They are always something special. We use them for parties or special occasions. In fact, we use them at Mass to remind us of how Jesus is present to us, like a light that makes us feel happy inside and is different from the ordinary ceiling lights. It is kind of like a new dawning, and that is what Jesus is to us. Let's just sit quietly for a few minutes now and look at the candles and think about how Jesus is like the candle and candlelight.

Gospel
   Let's stand now and listen to a story about Jesus and how he helped people see. Imagine yourself as the person in this story who comes up to Jesus.

Read the story of how Jesus cures the blind man. If appropriate, and with a small enough group, have children work in pairs. Blindfold half of them while others lead them around to touch objects, feel what it is like to walk in darkness, etc. This can be done as part of the homily.

Creed

Remember how St. Thomas said that he wouldn't believe Jesus unless he could see Him? It's like that with us. We have to see some things to believe them. We have to feel loved before we know what it is to love someone else. We have to learn to appreciate our gift of sight before we really begin to use it to look for prettiness and beauty in God's world. Today, let's pray the Creed and tell everybody what we believe because in some way we have seen it.

We believe in God our Father
because we see the beautiful things
in our world; and we believe that
things can be made better.
We believe in Jesus, our brother,
because we can see what happens when
we do as he said—
when we show love for one another.
We believe in the Spirit because we
can see the happiness and joy of
people who live with the Spirit of
Christianity. And we believe that
God keeps calling us to grow. We
believe that Jesus keeps asking us to
be like himself, to live for one another
and to sacrifice for one another and
to share each other's problems and
joys. We believe that the Spirit
keeps asking us to come together in
the Community of the Church and
live out what we believe. We believe
that together we can live and die and
come to the happiness which is
forever. Amen.

Offertory Prayer

All sing the following song, using the melody from the song From the Rising of the Sun.

From the rising of the sun,

even to its setting.
Your name is great among the nations
and everywhere we bring
sacrifice to your name.
Receive our bread, receive our wine,
and receive our coins and love for you
as we give praise. . . , and share our joy.

Preface
Priest: We have been with Jesus for such a long time, but still we do not know him. Since the day of our baptism he has not ceased to grow within us, to beautify his grace all the days of our lives.

Priest and children: But now our vision is cleared, our ears are opened, our hearts are lifted up, and we can join with the angels and saints to sing (say):
Song—*Morning Has Broken*

> *Ours is the sunlight,*
> *ours is the morning,*
> *as we praise Father,*
> *Jesus His Son.*
> *Praise Holy Spirit,*
> *praise God this morning,*
> *praise from creation,*
> *praise everyone.*

Canon
   The canon is recited by the priest. One of the approved canons should be used if this is a Eucharistic liturgy. Otherwise, the following is appropriate.

Priest: Lord, you are holy indeed, the fountain of all holiness and beauty. Let your spirit come upon these gifts to make them holy, so that they may become for us the body and blood of our Lord, Jesus Christ.
   Before he was given up to death, he took bread and gave you thanks. He broke the bread, gave it to his disciples, and said: "Take this, all of you, and eat it. This is my body which will be given up for you."
   When the supper was ended, he took the cup. Again he gave you thanks and praise, gave the cup to his disciples, and said: "Take this,

all of you, and drink from it. This is the cup of my blood, the blood of the new and everlasting covenant. It will be shed for you and for all men so that sins may be forgiven. Do this in memory of me."

Priest and children: (shouted, with gusto)

(clap!) *Glory be! Christ has died!*
(clap!) *Glory be! Christ is risen!*
(clap!) *Glory be! Christ comes again!*

Priest: And so Father, we remember Christ's death, his resurrection, his ascension, and his sending of the Holy Spirit. We rejoice in the gift of his love and presence in the world. Hidden God, clothed in your mystery, come among us; in this bread and this wine, come among us, in our hearts and in our lives. By the power of your Holy Spirit, break through and join us that we may celebrate your love and your peace and your strength.

Priest and Children: Orbit our lives with your Special Power, so that we may give you praise and honor and glory now and forever through Jesus Christ.

Song: *Yes Amen* by Robert Blue

The Lord's Prayer
Priest: With the eyes of our hearts focused on the signs of God's presence here among us, let us whisper to Christ the deepest prayer of our hearts:

Priest and children recite the Our Father using the ICEL text.

Priest: Deliver us Father, from every evil, and grant us peace this day. Banish all fear and anxiety from our lives, that we may live in the freedom of your way and light of your love.

Priest and children: For the kingdom, the power, and the glory are yours, now and forever. Amen.

Communion
Priest: Come brothers and sisters. Come, bursting of joy and smiles upon your faces. Receive the body of God, and celebrate his presence within you.

Prayer after Communion

Priest: We had come today, Lord, to put our business in order, to refresh our lives. And here we are involved in a new adventure. We wanted to see clearly your presence in bread and wine, but now we see you in everyone and in everyplace, waiting to greet us. Our zest for life is rekindled as we see with new eyes, hear with new ears, and feel with new hands, because your love is in us!

Priest and children: We have celebrated here together. Let us go in peace.

Priest: May the blessing of the Most High God, the Father, the Son, and the Holy Spirit, be upon you and remain with you.

Children: Song—*Peace My Friends* by Ray Repp

Note: The new Eucharistic Prayers for Children may be obtained by writing to: United States Catholic Conference, c/o Publications, 1312 Massachusetts Avenue, N.W., Washington, D.C. 20005

VIII
Worship
at
Church and Home

Going Home: Rediscovery and Defense of Family Liturgy

Michael E. Moynahan, S.J.

I. The Parish

As a child growing up in the fifties, I used to hear about the *cold war* between the United States and Russia and wonder what it was. You can experience it first hand in just about any Catholic church across the nation, during that part of the Mass known as the *kiss of peace*. This symbolic activity, which demands real physical involvement (actual touching!) and acknowledging the presence of that nameless Christian sitting next to you, is found disturbing, distasteful, and disruptive of what many consider prayer. And why? Precisely because this contact shatters the comfortable anonymity so many of us hide behind when we enter the insecure arena of communal worship known as liturgy.

How can you honestly expect a group of people who only see each other once a week to develop any feeling for that body next to them, let alone a sense of community? How can you expect them to pray together as members of one Christian family? How is what we do on Saturday nights and Sunday mornings possibly going to influence the quality of our lives together when our overriding feeling is that of relief when the *ordeal* known as Mass is over?

Much has been done in an effort to help the people worship together. I have seen some parishes effectively use the greeting, at the beginning of the Eucharistic celebration, as an opportunity for the people to introduce themselves to one another. It is important to chat for a few moments and hopefully know in some small—but not insignificant—way who those faces and bodies are worshipping to the right and left, in front of you and behind you. ("Close behind and close in front you fence me around, O Lord." Ps. 139)

All such efforts are commendable, but for the most part ineffective. The reason for this, I believe, is that our energy and our creativity are misdirected. We are trying to discover how to worship more effectively and are unwittingly being confronted with the problem that underlies it. We are dealing with the problem of the composition and definition of the parish.

And what is the parish? Generally, it is a group of people expected to worship as a family or community who do little or nothing else together except congregate one day a week. During the time they are together, they hear the good news (?), share the Lord's supper, pay their *fair share,* and through this all maintain a respectful distance and healthy anonymity. A person who finds himself in a parish usually has little else in common with a given group of people other than the fact that they all reside within the same arbitrary geographical confines known in ecclesiastical jargon as a *parish.*

Is there little wonder, then, why parishes are experiencing problems? Or why, in fact, the parish structure is breaking down? Why will people travel great distances to participate in a liturgy outside of their parish? I have experienced this wherever I have gone. This has been the case at the Brophy College Prep Chapel in Phoenix, Arizona. The same is true of other such places like the Franciscan Retreat House in Scottsdale, Arizona, and St. Francis de Sales Cathedral parish in Oakland, California. Do the people travel great distances because these places put on *good shows* or have *groovy* liturgies? Or could it be that they find it easier to worship with these particular groups of people? Could it be that they feel more comfortable and have more in common with these ungeographically defined but congregated groups? I feel most people's reasons fall under these last two headings. Because of this, the liturgies meet more their concrete need for the Eucharistic celebration to be not only the sacrament and sign of their unity, but the very means by which they strengthen and support that unity with fellow worshipping Christians.

I think the liturgical problems experienced on the parish level are understandable and human ones. Why? Well, think for a moment. What is the most natural unit you can think of? What group of people do you have most in common with? With whom do you come together and share most? Is it your parish? Could it be your diocese? Maybe it's some social club? Or perhaps it's your block? Or is it, after all is said and done, your family? I think, for most, the answer is their family. The family is certainly the most natural unit. It is also the smallest and most workable unit.

Just reflect on your own experience. Would you take a vacation with a complete stranger? You might, but you'd probably be pretty uncomfortable. Some vacation! With whom do you share the good things that happen in your life? For whom do you like to do things, buy things, and be of service? The answers to all of the above questions are people whom you know and love. Probably for most of us, this would be our families—either natural or acquired.

Now another question. With whom do you pray or share an intimate part of yourself? With whom do you share the Word of God and the supper of the Lord? Outside of the few members who make up our different families, the answer is either the futile "I have no control over that," or the honest fact—"strangers." And you know something? It's pretty hard to share something personal and intimate with strangers.

If we enter a liturgy strangers, chances are we will leave the liturgy strangers, confirmed in this particular liturgy's *strangeness*. You simply cannot build *instant community*. Consequently, you are not going to have spontaneously good liturgy. Community and family take time to build. It is a very painful and only too human process. The same can and must be said about liturgy. How often have we stumbled through all those awkward liturgical attempts to witness to and build a *community* that does not exist and cannot exist? These attempts can become gimmicks and devices when one of the primary things we are not celebrating is the unity that already exists—however imperfectly—among us.

II. Liturgy

Fundamentally, I believe we are a liturgical people. Ritualized activity is a very basic and important part of our life. There are patterns of activity and repetition in our lives out of our concrete need for them, not out of boredom. We need a certain amount of routine in what we do, not because we are dull, unimaginative people, but because we crave ritualized activity that adds a dimension of meaning to our lives.

When we attend a football game, play golf or bridge, go to the symphony or get off to the beach for a weekend, there are certain things we bring to these experiences and encounters—attitudes as well as objects—that make things happen and charge these experiences with special meaning for us. It really wouldn't have been an authentic celebration at my house, every year on my birthday, if mother had not made an angel food cake with Philadelphia Cream Cheese icing. Thanksgiving would never have been the same if we had eaten chicken and dumplings instead of turkey with all the trimmings. Can you imagine stringing lights on a Christmas egg instead of a Christmas tree? So, there is much activity in our lives that is repetitious for a reason. And we call this ritual.

What, then, is liturgy? Perhaps we can spend a few moments explaining what we mean when we use the word liturgy. The word liturgy is made up of two words: one meaning people, and the other signifying work, service or office. So the fundamental meaning of liturgy is activity performed not for private ends, but for the sake of the people. In scripture, the word was a technical term for the worship of the people and has remained so through the centuries, finally being specially applied to the Eucharist.

There is a pattern of activity in liturgy. There is also a certain amount of repetition. Liturgy is always worship. It is prayer, and is directed to God the Father. It is a prayer of praise to God for all the ways he is Father to us. It is a prayer of thanksgiving to God for the Father's love he showers upon us through all his gifts.

And what is the relationship between liturgy and ritual? Like many of the other ritualized activities in our lives, we experience a need and a desire for liturgy. We need the opportunity to thank God for being God and giving us the gifts of self and others. We need the opportunity to become more conscious of the presence of God in our lives and our world. Liturgy can not only challenge our consciousness, but provide us with the precious time of reflection and contemplation needed to once again come into contact with this vital presence. We also need the chance to try and express our reaction, to make concrete in sign and act our response. We do this ritually in liturgical prayer.

One of the patterns found in liturgy is that it is done together. Liturgy is communal prayer. It is the prayer experience of the community. The early Christians gathered together not in the temples of Judaism but in one another's homes, where they heard the scriptures proclaimed and shared the meal in memory of Jesus Christ. They celebrated liturgically the unity that as a community they brought to it, and experienced in that very worship an increased development and strengthening of that unity. They were bound closer together in faith, word and sacrament.

It is important to remember that liturgy is not simply some pious private devotion. Liturgy involves the important and dramatic as we experience the presence of God in community. In liturgy, we join together not just as individuals, but as members of one family. And as a family, together we praise and thank Our Father for the ways he is present to us—especially in the way he has drawn us together in community.

III. The Family

I have been tossing the word *family* about rather freely. Perhaps it would be good to try and pin it down a little. When you use the word *family* it's hard to be precise, for we have many families. There is the family we are born into which consists of mother, father, brothers and sisters. This might be called our natural family. Our cousins, aunts, uncles, nieces, nephews, and grandparents are also part of that natural family. So they are distinguished by referring to them as distant family as opposed to mothers, fathers, etc., who then become immediate family. The people who live on the same block might form another family. Business associates, school buddies, club members and other friends might form yet another family. In the broadest sense, our family is the group of people with whom we are bound together by a sharing of communal interests, attitudes and goals. Families are groups of people who share one heart and one spirit. They work not simply to preserve self-interests, but for the unity and good of the whole.

It is important that we learn to work and share with all our different types of families. The more all members co-operate, the better the chances for our families becoming powerful instruments for good. Now I will be using *family* mostly in the sense of our natural immediate family. But this is a primary emphasis. It does not exclude our other types of families.

I also realize the difficulties some immediate families have living and sharing together. It can be hard for them to love one another and work not simply as individuals but as a unified whole. Nevertheless, I believe that the home is the most natural place to become a family and build community. And it is in the home that we find the most common source of experience and natural occasions to celebrate liturgically.

Now the family is the paradigm or model for most institutional units, including the Church. In the family, all members work together for the good of the whole. The family is an example of St. Paul's analogy of the body found in his first letter to the Corinthians. There are indeed a variety of gifts, but only one Spirit supplying those gifts. There are many parts to the body, but the body needs the co-operation of every part to be a real, complete and healthy body. There are different members of each family, but all must learn to love one another and work together in order for the family to grow and develop and share with others the unique gifts that they have received. We, the Church, are called to be a family that has one common Father. We who are many are called to be one. We demonstrate and celebrate this unity in liturgy. But we can only be a family of brothers and sisters working together in the Church of Jesus Christ if we have learned the lesson of familial co-operation in our many homes.

We are able to gather together to celebrate and worship as a

Church in direct proportion to our ability to gather together, celebrate and worship as a family. We cannot give what we do not have. We cannot share or bring to church what we have not found and experienced in our families.

Does liturgy build unity, family, and community? Or does it presuppose it? Actually, the answer lies somewhere in between these two poles. We cannot celebrate what is not there, at least in some stage. But we do not remain unchanged because of what we do. We are, in liturgy, caught up in a process. We are continually growing more into the complete family of God we one day hope to be. Our desire to be one brings us together. And we celebrate not only the fact that God calls us all to be one, but a unity that already exists however imperfectly. It is as a family that we grow in and share one faith, one hope, one love and Lord in Jesus Christ. And we celebrate this in liturgy.

Many religious communities used to liturgize at different times of the day. They used to keep the liturgy of *hours*. Religious men and women would gather together to praise and thank God as a religious family. Liturgy, communal worship, familial thanksgiving and praise to God for being our Father and calling us together in community is not just the assigned duty of a few religious communities. All Christian families are called by God to discover and share his love in community, and together to gratefully return thanksgiving and praise. We can do this in many ways. We do it best in liturgy, especially family liturgy.

IV. Family Liturgy

Family liturgy can be taken in two senses. In the narrowest sense, we can speak of a family liturgy as a home Eucharist, a familial celebration of the Lord's supper. But this is only one type of family liturgy. Or we can speak of family liturgy in the broader sense, of all those people, occasions and events that flow from the experience of family and cry out to be celebrated liturgically.

I have found all the home Eucharists I have participated in very moving and profitable experiences. I discovered dimensions of my brothers, sisters, parents, family and friends that I had not experienced before. Our worship became very reflective of our communal and familial concerns. It was easy to thank God for gifts we had received, gifts we were all aware of and had shared with each other. It was easy to do this thanksgiving in a spirit of confidence and trust. There is tremendous security in knowing you are with people who know you, who free you, with whom you do not have to be afraid or couch your words for fear of misunderstanding, or qualify things out of existence for fear of offending someone's sensibilities. It was easy, in these home situations, to confidently put our needs and concerns before the Lord and ask the prayerful support of the other members of this believing and worshipping community.

And what are some of the other types of family liturgies? Well, it is in the home that the most natural situations arise for giving thanks to God our Father as a family. It is important to capitalize on all such occasions and familial events that offer the possibility of ritualization through a home liturgy other than the Eucharist. Some of these occasions and events might be: a birthday in the family, moving into a new home, a child leaving home for the first time to attend school, celebrating any number of your children's discoveries (e.g., tying his shoes by himself for the first time, or discovering any of the wonders of creation), a family service of forgiveness or reconciliation after fallings out or misunderstandings, a liturgy during a member of the family's illness, the blessing of the food at the evening meal, or special dinner blessings when family and friends are gathered on special occasions like Thanksgiving, Christmas, Easter or Independence Day. The liturgical possibilities are only limited by our own creativity and imagination.

The home, therefore, is a natural liturgical environment that provides countless natural liturgical situations. And why not? For it is in the family that we share a common experience with one another. Family is a small community. It is here that we experience the presence and love of God first. It should also be in this same environment, with the family, that we first learn to thank God for all his gifts and love to us.

V. Conclusion

Liturgy is a proclamation/response event. Under what circumstances can we respond most fully and most freely? This will give us a good idea of the atmosphere and environment we should look for and strive to provide to enable the best possible liturgical experience.

The aim of good liturgy is to involve the worshipers as fully as possible. The more complete the participation, the greater the possibilities of the liturgical experience. Now, where would you feel freest to participate or respond? Would you feel free to involve yourself, fully put yourself into worship where you are surrounded by strangers? If liturgy were just a God and me event, there might not be any problems. But liturgy is a God and we event. It is a communitarian religious experience. We cannot ignore the other in liturgy, for without them there can be no liturgy.

So, can we worship surrounded by strangers? Psychologists and sociologists would label this type of environment as unknown or hostile. Even the strongest character would find difficulty participating fully or profitably in this type of environment. The family and home, then, would seem to be the most natural place to participate fully and freely. And the family and home are by far the most important place for sharing on a liturgical level to take place.

If we would revitalize our liturgy, we must not simply look to our churches. We must look to the family and our homes. In rediscovering and developing the liturgical opportunities that arise out of our family situations, we can tremendously contribute to the enrichment of our church liturgical experience. Let us be realistic in our appraisal of what is present and what is lacking in our church liturgical experience. And then let us hopefully investigate and experiment with all the liturgical possibilities that come from the home. We need our liturgy. And our liturgy needs to be revitalized. So let us begin by going home.

Celebrating at Home

John P. Mossi, S.J.

And day by day, attending the temple together and breaking bread in their homes, *they partook of food with glad and generous hearts. Acts 2:46.*

The modern family is surprised or sometimes embarrassed to find out that worship for the early Church constituted part of everyone's daily pattern. Not only did they worship "day by day," but one of their settings was the home! Perhaps Acts 2:46 is a subtle indication of where the contemporary Church is in need of religious growth.

For years teachers have cried out that learning doesn't end at school but has to be supported and complemented in the home. The same principle applies to worship. There is a basic relationship between celebrating with one's own family and then, with the larger community, the Church. The early Christians developed their home worship services which in turn enriched their larger community gatherings. Catechesis, prayer, and liturgical worship were part of the total fabric of the home environment.

Does the worship of the early Church say anything about the importance of worship in the home today? It certainly does if Sunday worship is to remain a valid and meaningful religious experience. We often think of our parish church as *that old stone building around the corner,* instead of as it really is: a community of believers, the People of God. It is essential that this worshiping community receive nourishment from the family unit. Why? The church at worship is really the extension of the prayer-life of the home. A family who can pray together will also be able to comfortably pray with other families. The result for the church is a People of God actively contributing to the quality of the community's worship. For the family, intimacy with worship and prayer brings increased meaning to liturgical actions, whether this might be the sign of the cross or a simple bowing of the head. In time, the family becomes familiar with church symbolism as found in vestments or in the colors of liturgical seasons. A family that worships at home is as much at home at church. Sunday worship is not reduced to what it is for many of us: a special T.V. channel that is tuned in for one hour each week and then turned off. Home and church, for their own mutual meaning and survival, must be organically intertwined.

What is necessary for a family to worship together? Here are a few rules that seem to work: (1) the whole family, not just the parents, or the children, should creatively participate; (2) next, a place and a special time for prayer are set aside that are fastidiously respected by all; (3) initially this time should be relatively short, between five to ten minutes.

There are countless ways a family may worship together. Many have found the most convenient setting for family prayer is just before the evening meal. A few growling stomachs might have to be held in control, but the attempt and its success are certainly worth the initial pangs.

Here is a simple pre-supper celebration that can be easily adapted to each family's preferences. While everyone is standing around the table, begin with a reverent sign of the cross. This deliberate action helps to slow down the hectic pace of the day, making one receptive for prayer. Next, a special blessing for the family is spontaneously said. A different member of the family can take responsibility in leading this blessing each night.

When everyone is seated, another member reads a section from the Bible. This can be a continuous reading from one of the gospels, psalms, prophets, or an anticipation of the readings for the coming Sunday. A period follows the reading offering an opportunity to respond in silence or in prayer to the proclaimed Word. At the appropriate time, hands are joined as a concrete gesture of unity and the Our Father recited. The exposed Bible is then positioned in a suitable resting place or perhaps on a nearby mantle. Through this simple worship exercise, the dinner table has taken on new meaning. It is the table of spiritual nourishment as well.

The manner in which the table is decorated is also important for conveying a prayerful atmosphere as well as teaching about Church symbolism. As our prayers represent our inmost desires and hopes, so can an attractive arrangement convey the same meaning expressed in a different form. For example, a candle can be lit followed by a short prayer expressing our need of Christ to illuminate our lives.

Heavenly Father, with the lighting of this candle, remind us of our dependence on the words and example of Jesus who is the Light of the World.

The symbolism of the candle can be further enhanced by having it correspond to the liturgical color of the season: red representing the tongues of fire of the Holy Spirit for Pentecost Sunday, purple which is a color of penitence for Lent, green meaning growth in the Spirit for the season of Pentecost, white which recalls the radiance of the risen Christ, gold a color honoring the Prince of Peace during the Christmas season. For the sake of variety, flowers, a drawing, a statue, a paper cutout, or other easy-to-make table decorations are excellent substitutes. On occasion, holy water can be used as a reminder of everyone's baptism into the family of God and rebirth in the life of the Spirit.

Especially if a family is blessed with children, their spontaneity and innocence mixed with humor can be a source of inspiration. Children are great teachers for they help adult eyes to see the common and ordinary with fresh light and new vision. Moreover, they are unafraid to pray about their personal experiences with their friends and express their cares and concerns with simpleness and pureness of heart. And this quality needs to be capitalized on and developed.

Families who have been praying together for some time refer to this period of the day as a joy. For some it is the joy of encountering once again the consoling Word of God as experienced in a different section of the Bible or perhaps receiving a new insight into a familiar gospel narrative. Others have felt a closer bond of union in the family because during home worship members readily pray for one another and ask forgiveness for their failings. Still others speak of a tighter unity between the worship experience of home and church. What is important is that prayer is no longer a private or a foreign activity but one that is experienced by the whole family. One of the benefits is the lessening of distance between the home table and the Table of the Lord, which is one's parish altar. Prayer and worship, as in the days of the early Church, take place at both.

As ease develops with the practice of communal prayer in the home, the time, format, and setting of prayer will naturally change. Favorite family sites such as a beach, a forest, a campfire, a hilltop, a waterfall also invite prayer in their own special way. Families can celebrate the approach of summer or snow, a holiday or an engagement, the refreshing coolness of water or a beautiful sunset. God is present in all of creation and so the list and the possibilities for family worship are really endless.

Realistically, the problem that most families encounter in establishing the practice of family worship is in the beginning. The first few attempts will understandably be awkward, with feelings of uneasiness in starting something new. Learning to worship together is like diving into a lake; the initial plunge into the water must be taken at some time. Otherwise the joy of swimming is never experienced. So why not try praying together this week? Or better yet, today? The families who have done so have happily found family worship a supporting and mutually enriching experience of the presence and goodness of God.

There are several books that are available as aids for family worship. Supreme on the list is the Bible. Many families still don't possess a copy of the Bible; its presentation to the family can be the occasion for using it at table. Here are a few versions to fit your particular style. *The Living Bible* is a new paraphrased version written in colloquial English with modern imagery and examples used in its parables and stories. *The New American Bible* renders a more literal translation. *The Jerusalem Bible* has a poetic flare, brief introductions to the various books, and marginal cross-references to the verses.

There are other books that are helpful for the planning of family worship. *Parish and Families* published by the Liturgical Conference is a very comprehensive book that follows the general cycle of the Church year, providing creative ideas on how to celebrate the seasons and the major feasts of the Church in the setting of one's home.

Wonder and Worship of Newman Press is a book of original fairy tales for the young of age and the young at heart. After each story, a scripture text and theme are suggested that either complement or contrast the fairy tale. This book is ideal for a long night by a fireplace.

Celebrate Summer! published by Paulist Press takes the ordinary summer experiences of air, water, fire, sunshine or days like Labor Day, Independence Day, Memorial Day and provides very imaginative ways of finding and celebrating God's presence in them.

All the necessary ingredients are now before you in order to discover and create your own family worship. Go ahead and try. Plunge into the water. You will find that as the grace of the Spirit was ever present to the families of the early Church, his peace and joy will also be with yours.

Festival Focus on Family

Adeline Kroll, O.S.F.

Sr. Kroll has many years of experience with elementary and secondary education in Minnesota. Her forte is adapting and creating liturgies for children and families.

How many things, events, persons can be celebrated in a family? Somehow the beauty of a deeper dimension can be added when we integrate celebration with a prayer experience. A birthday-life celebration, a forgiveness celebration, or a family listening together to see where God is leading them, can strengthen bonds and give a new enthusiasm and sensitivity in responding to the gift of life.

Through the new rite of Baptism the parents are called to bring their child to an awareness of God acting in the life of the child, and the whole family to facilitate a faith response in that child. With the discovery of God's action and presence in the daily events of eating, searching, belonging, caring, seeking support, crying, encouraging, . . . each person comes to a response to that God who calls from them a commitment and a surrender in love.

How do we come to that faith response in a family? First we must realize that God is already acting and speaking to us. We are already coming together at different times in each day. Within this fellowship of the family we can listen and respond to God. Our religious experience always depends on the commitment with which we surrender to the Father. In a prayer experience we merely ritualize things from our daily experience.

Praise is a response to an awareness that God is acting. To draw awareness from daily events we must first discover *who we are* today. Are we in a birthday celebration mood? Are we saddened at misunderstandings in our family? Are we lonely because sickness separates us from friends or family? Are we preparing to celebrate an event that will bring us together as a group?

Next we must determine the best way to *express* who we are. If the coming together is one of festivity, then ask yourself, "What would express that best?" If it is popcorn balls, pulling taffy, having a birthday cake, sharing the gifts each person has, or spending time with a sick or lonely person, then move in the direction that calls forth a fitting response.

We do have a need to come together. When we come together, we have some things that need to be done or said. It may help to set up a ritual context in which we can place those necessary expressions.

A family ritual celebration should have a beginning, a middle, and an end. It should be short if there are some children who are too small to appreciate a long prayer. (This is *for* the family, not *in spite of* the family!) Many structures are possible, and one suggested structure for family celebration might be:

Opening Song: This can be a favorite song that sets a mood related to the feelings or need that draws the family together.

Opening Prayer: One of the family members can summarize the event or happening that is being celebrated.

Reading: Perhaps a scripture reading which expresses the *message* in our action. This helps to identify our family experience with God's forming word.

Activity: Discussion of the reading, or spontaneous prayers from the family members, relating the significance of the event according to their ability to understand the relationship. Sharing these insights among older and younger members of the family encourages growth through each other.

Closing Prayer or Song: This brings the ritual to an end.

The most rewarding celebrations are ones that are planned and conceived by the family itself. To get you started though, here are some examples.

PEACE AND RECONCILIATION

Opening Song: Prayer of Saint Francis

.Opening Prayer: Jesus, you are truly a Son of God, the Prince of Peace, the peacemaker who reaches out to lift up the needy and the poor to heal. Strengthen and show them love. Let us walk with you down the road of mercy and kindness, asking forgiveness and forgiving, that love may be for all men. Amen.

Activity: Light a candle (to remind all that Christ is the light of the world, and is present among us).

    1. Read headlines from a newspaper. Pray for the causes in the world that need God's mercy to bring peace into them. (Response: Lord have mercy!)

    2. Ask forgiveness for some ways each person causes hurt or ruins the peace in the family. (Response: Lord have mercy.)

Closing Prayer: Lord, we praise you for coming to our home. Make our hearts leap with gladness and tip-toe with the wonder of a man called Jesus, who dared to come as a gift to the world, so all men could come together as brothers. We can now stand on street corners and shout cheery wishes to strangers because Jesus has made us to know that the Father loves us. Fill us with your peace. Amen.

CELEBRATE BEING A FAMILY

Opening Song: Kumbaya

Reading: Col. 3:12-21

Activity: Discuss what it means to be a Christian family, as a commitment sign to Christ and to help each other:

1. Light a candle.
2. Join hands around the light.
3. State goals, intentions, needs, things for which help is needed. (Response: We will help you do this. Or, Father, hear our prayer.)

Closing Prayer: Our Father

Closing Song: A family favorite.

EATING TOGETHER

Beforehand: Personally invite each member of the family to the meal.

Opening Song: When the Saints Go Marching In

Reading: Matthew 22:1-14

Activities: Discuss or act out the scripture reading. What does it mean to eat together? What does it mean to us to have a family to enjoy? How does God call on our family to serve him? What is one thing we can do to show our response to God for his goodness?

Prayer: Amen. Thank you. Yes. That's what I have to say to you, Lord. It's overflowing from all good happenings that tell me you care for me and watch over me. May *thank you* and *yes* come from the heart of all people as they reach out to you. May all peoples find your work in each other and proclaim it from the housetop.

CELEBRATE THE LORD'S DAY

Reading: Genesis 1:26-31

Prayer: Make a litany of thanks for the goodness of God to you not only on the Lord's day, but every day. (Response: Lord, we thank you!)

Activities:

1. Take a short trip as a family. On the trip point out to each other the many beautiful things created by God for man to enjoy. Are there some that can't be seen?
2. How does your family remember the goodness of God on His day? Can you do something this Sunday to bring special delight to each other? Perhaps create a play, pull taffy, make a cake, go on a special visit, or just reminisce together.
3. Take someone to Mass this Sunday who cannot get there without help, such as an older person imprisoned due to age, ice, snow, distance, etc.

Thanksgiving for Gifts

Prayer: Lord, you call us together as your people that we may come to know and love you as we serve each other in Christ. Open our hearts to your way so that we may care and dare to make your message of Good News for all men grow in our family, and in the family of all mankind.

Reading: 1 Cor. 12:4-11

Activity: Wrap a gift package, and imagine it as your talent or gift to the family. Have the others guess what it is. Then explain what you thought of it as. How is your gift to the family shared?

Closing Prayer: Our Father

Closing Song: All That I Am

Discover Life

Opening Prayer: Lord, it is no little thing to lay down your life for love. You make an old people into a new people of God, a frightened people into a quiet and forgiven people. We come to you giving ourselves as a gift in response to your love.

Reading: John 12:20-33. Jesus uses a beautiful symbol of love, a relationship which requires a total gift of himself. According to the reading, how is a grain of wheat like the giving of one's life to the worship and service of God?

Activity: Think of ways that God has blessed your life. Tell the others.

Each person think of some way to give himself or herself to God. (This can be done in a moment of silence.)

Each take a glass of juice and pour it into a large container while saying out loud what will be offered to God.

When everyone has joined in the offering, refill the glasses from the large container and share in the offering of each other.

Closing Prayer: Our Father.

Closing Song: All That I Am.

The Family Shrine

James Notebaart

The concept of the family shrine or prayer area actually precedes the building of churches. It even predates Christianity. We would normally expect to find Christian practices stemming from Jewish ones. However, the origin of the home shrine cannot be found in Judaism. For the Jewish law prohibiting divine images effectively eliminated the possibility of special image areas. The Jewish family prayer centered around the dining table, and the visual elements which accompanied the prayer, such as the seven-branch candlestick, the Isaiah cup, the Chanukkah lamps, were temporary elements rather than a form of shrine.

We might find the origin of the shrine in the Roman pagan tradition, however. For the Romans had household gods, a goddess of the hearth, Vesta; and Janus, the god of good beginnings. They revered family ancestors and other deified humans such as the emperors. In fact, they had special places for these deities. The higher gods had niches in the walls and the lower ones had pedestals. There were wall paintings as well which depicted the lives and adventures of their gods. These were colorful and often filled whole wall areas.

As more and more Romans became Christian, we find more Roman practices creeping into Christianity. The paintings of the gods soon became Biblical scenes. In England and Dura-Europos in Asia Minor, two house-churches have been found which date to the third century. These have Biblical scenes painted on the walls, these paintings set off special areas of the houses. In England they seem to have been in a room for liturgy. In Dura-Europos the paintings were in an entry space. The adaptation from the Roman pagan tradition is clear.

The Roman niches and pedestals may have been used for reservation of the Eucharist. For it was an early Christian practice to bring the Eucharist home for daily reception. We find references to the practice in Hippolitus' work, *The Apostolic Tradition* (LXXVII-VIII) dating to about 215 A.D. It was in Tertullian's work *De Spectaculis* (V) dating to about 200 A.D. that he warned the Christians to care for the Eucharist properly. It would have been a logical step to keep the Eucharist in a special place even as the Roman gods had been kept. We have some evidence that this may be true, for archaeologists found a cupboard with a cross-shaped indentation above it at Pompeii (ca. A.D. 79). This would have been a consistent Roman usage for the gods and prayer.

We do not have clear evidence of statuary in the Christian homes, however. There is an Appollo-Christ figure in the Vatican Museum which dates to the first few centuries, but we do not know how it was used nor where it was placed.

Following the Roman period there is a long and clear history of shrines in the homes. In Germany there was the *Hellgottskuchel,* the *Bright Corner of the Lord.* This area was found at the corner of the building, and the crucified Christ was carved in the supporting vertical and horizontal beams of the house. So it was literally the Lord who was the physical support of the home. This area was decorated with fresh flowers, etc. It was a place where one could go to encounter the Lord in some visual way. This corner was a tangible witness to the faith of the family as well.

The shrines in Greece centered around the icon (a painting of Jesus or Mary or one of the saints). The icon was often painted by one of the members of the family but in certain traditional styles so that there was a visual continuity between all Christian homes. The icon hung on the wall and there was an oil lamp burning in front of it. The lamp was a witness to the continual attention of the family, for the lamp had to be refueled each day. Like the German shrine there is a sense of continuous use and daily care.

In the Philippine Islands the shrines often were modeled after the Spanish statuary. The kitchen seemed to be the place where they appeared. The statues of saints or Our Lord were placed on shelves and treated similarly to the German tradition.

What is important to note in all three styles is that there was no attempt to make the shrine a little church. The shrines were not altars. In fact, the tradition is Roman so *altar* is not an appropriate origin for the shrine. Secondly the shrines were not merely decorative like the Last Supper in some dining rooms. But they were places of regular prayer. The shrines were centers of prayer like the table is the center of family prayer in Judaism.

The original purpose of the shrine area was practical. It was a place to keep the Eucharist in the home. This practice has not been revived, although it could be, if one brought daily communion to the ill. The shrine was also meant to be a living witness to anyone who entered the house. It is meant to give others a measure by which to gauge the lives of the family. Are their lives compatible with the sentiments of the shrine? The shrine is meant to say: "We have a living concern, a daily concern about the Lord's place in our life." This represents the conviction that Christianity is a visible reality as well as a spiritual one.

A few years ago our concepts of prayer broadened until finally we said: *Everything* is prayer. If that was true, we needed no visual spaces for prayer. But we found that, if *everything* is prayer, then we soon lost tangible contact with the Lord. Now we are reevaluating this attitude, and we find both are important. We must live lives of prayer but we should set aside special times and places to deepen our understanding of the Lord's presence in our life. The shrine becomes the *tangible* touchstone for our lived faith. It helps us recognize the world which stands before us, and it helps us to become aware and sensitive to that world. The shrine acts as a catalyst by introducing lasting values in an ephemeral world. The flowers that die and the oil that is consumed are virtual symbols of our life in its fragile beauty.

The shrine most of all is a place where we can encounter the Lord, where we can be with him alone, or where the family can share prayer together and grow. The purpose of the shrine must lead to a deeper community prayer. It must direct us to the worship in the Church. Vatican Council II sets guidelines for us in its *Constitution on the Liturgy*. It says: "Popular devotions of the Christian people are warmly commended, provided they are in accord with the laws and norms of the Church. . . . These devotions should be so drawn up that they harmonize with the liturgical seasons, accord with the sacred liturgy, and in some fashion are derived from it and lead the people to it." (No. 13.)

There are a few cautions about shrines, however. In suggesting shrines, the key element to be observed is that the shrines are not to be meaningless. If they are just decorations, they are not serving the function for which they are made. Secondly, good taste is important. In Germany, in Greece and in the Philippine Islands the shrines were simple: one major image with changeable flowers, etc. Good taste is the criterion that will give a wholesome sense of the Lord. The icon, the engraving, the simple cross say more than a plaster-painted statue. Even children's drawings are often more perceptive than some commercial piece of *sacred art*. What is culturally cheap and ostentatious cannot deepen our relationship with the Lord.

Theology is another important factor in creating a viable shrine. If the picture of the Lord is effeminate, what image do we have of him? If Mary is not related to her place as Mother of the Lord and believing member of the Church, then again we have misdirected ourselves. It is in the liturgy that we look for our theology of the Lord and His Church. Jesus is Lord, powerful, risen, loving, and our brother. In Greece, for instance, the only image of the Resurrection was the sun. So Jesus is most often portrayed as dressed in gold or orange. When the light strikes the icon, it is aglow—warm and rich. This is one example of the form which expressed a theological point; namely, the Resurrection. The form the shrine takes will express its theological sentiment. So we should be aware of what we are saying.

Shrines can be thematic and temporary. There is no reason why they have to be permanent. There are certain key times in the liturgical cycle—Advent, Lent, Easter—when we might want to make a visible place for prayer. In fact, we might even want to relate it to the table as the Jews did, rather than to a corner or on a wall. If we can make the seasons more alive in our homes, we can make them more alive in worship. How our place of prayer looks or what it is made of should come from the family rather than be imposed on them. If we make the table a prayer place for certain meals, then the whole family should decide how to make it work. Rather than buying a candle, for instance, make a candle. Rather than buying figures, make them out of straw. Maybe a mounted picture drawn by one of the children and hung above the table would set off the table as a special place.

If we choose a place such as a wall or corner, we should use the guidelines of Germany, Greece and the Philippine Islands. The place, above all, should be an authentic place of prayer rather than an affectation.

For myself, the concept of the corner of the Lord really works. It was about ten years ago that I first heard about it. I thought I would see if it did anything for my prayer life. For a long time, as I look back at it now, it was an artificial place. I did too much. Gradually I simplified my concept until it was merely a cross; sometimes I lit a candle when I prayed. Lent meant a bowl of dry sticks and a simplified home. Easter was an Easter lily in front of the cross.

I once had a friend who was dying of cancer, so I bought a seven-day sanctuary candle and everytime I awakened I saw the glow, and I remembered her suffering. Today my prayer place is a place I can be with the Lord. It is austere, simple, far from sentimental, an icon of the Resurrection.

What is more important than the form it took is that I have decided to set aside a place. I have a *place* of prayer in my home.